Just Deserts for Corporate Criminals

Kip Schlegel

JUST DESERTS FOR CORPORATE CRIMINALS

Boston

NORTHEASTERN UNIVERSITY PRESS

Northeastern University Press 1990

Library of Congress Cataloging-in-Publication Data

Schlegel, Kip.
Just deserts for corporate criminals / Kip Schlegel.
p.   cm.
Includes bibliographical references.
ISBN 1–55553–076–1
1. Criminal liability of juristic persons—United States.
2. Corporation law—United States—Criminal provisions.
3. Sentences (Criminal procedure)—United States.   I. Title.
KF9236.5.S35   1990
345.73′0268—dc20
[347.305268]   90–31207
CIP

Designed by David Ford
Composed in Caledonia by BookMasters, Ashland, Ohio.
Printed and bound by BookCrafters, Chelsea, Michigan.
The paper is Glatfelter Offset, an acid-free sheet.

MANUFACTURED IN THE UNITED STATES OF AMERICA
95   94   93   92   91   90   5   4   3   2   1

IN MEMORY

Richard Franklin Sparks

Contents

Contents

Preface

Did you ever expect a corporation to have a conscience,
when is has no soul to be damned,
and no body to be kicked?

Edward, First Baron Thurlow

A GOOD AMOUNT of what is called the "news" has recently involved the criminal acts of large corporations. Corporate crime is often depicted as an emerging crisis, a problem growing in exponential fashion. In reality, however, there is nothing emergent about it at all. Since the inception of the modern corporation, there have been entities that have violated the criminal law, often repeatedly. Nor is there anything unique about the harms resulting from more recent corporate crimes that would set them apart from the deaths and injuries wrought by corporate criminality in earlier days. What recent corporate offense can surpass the harm caused by the drug Thalidomide that occurred in the late 1950s? Nearly eight thousand children (approximately half the number of those who died at birth as a result of the drug) remain alive, many without arms and legs. The memory continues to haunt us.

It is therefore difficult to trace the causes for the recent surge of interest in corporate crime. Nonetheless, one of the inevitable by-products of the publicity is the concern about corporate punishment. Echoes of Lord Thurlow's complaint resound. Can the criminal sanction have any impact on "soulless" entities that cannot "feel" the effects of the condemnation and hard treatment that punishment represents?

This issue has not escaped the interest of scholars who think about corporate transgressions. Indeed, to its credit, the media's attention to corporate misconduct over the past decade has helped to rekindle an interest among criminologists, economists, sociologists, and corporate legal theorists about the problems of corporate crime and punishment.

The focus of a great part of the recent scholarly literature on corporate punishment has a decidedly deterrent (crime-control) cast. Much of it has concentrated on the feasibility, or lack thereof, of deterrence as it applies to large organizational settings and to individuals whose actions are in part determined by the structural forces and constraints that exist within large corporations. Much of the effort has been directed toward ways to maximize the imposition of the criminal sanction to bolster crime control, as well as toward locating the optimal deterrent points in the allocation of corporate punishments. Yet, proposed solutions have been found wanting.

However, crime control is not the only function of the criminal sanction, nor is deterrence or any other crime-control rationale the only principle upon which corporate punishments may be allocated. A retributive rationale, which looks to the institution of punishment as representing the reflection of moral condemnation of the crime and the perpetrator by society, has largely been ignored. More important, the application of desert principles (commonly referred to as just deserts), which mandate that the quantum of punishment reflect fairly the seriousness of the offense, has been virtually discounted altogether. From a desert perspective, seriousness is determined on the basis of the harm caused or risked by the act and the culpability of the actor. Offenses of equal seriousness merit equal punishment, and changes in the severity of the punishment should correspond directly to the changes in relative seriousness of the offense.

This book is an attempt to fill a void in the scholarship on corporate punishment. It represents a theoretical examination of the application of desert principles to the punishment of corporations and their agents. It examines both the general rationale for desert in the context of corporate criminality and the specific problems that confront a desert-based system of corporate punishment.

The neglect of desert theory by corporate legal theorists can be summarized in the following claims. First, it is argued that retribution is not applicable as a justification for corporate criminal sanctions because such retributive concepts as vengeance and Kantian notions of the restoration of benefits and burdens make no sense in the realm of corporate crime. Second, desert, which focuses on the concept of blame, is inapplicable with regard to corporate offenses that are regulatory and not considered morally wrong. Third, any principle that focuses on blame is inappropriate in the corporate context since corporations as entities do not have a conscience, by which alone the concept of blame makes sense.

The first half of the book is directed toward these issues. It begins with an examination of recent punishment practices. Because the rationale for sentencing often takes its form from the rationale for the criminal sanction in general, the evolution of corporate and individual liability in the corporate context is briefly examined. This is followed by a review of various enforcement strategies and some tentative explanations that have been suggested as to their use. Because the focus of corporate sentencing is on crime control, a critique of the deterrent effectiveness of corporate criminal sanctions will also be considered.

These chapters are followed by a general discussion of the evolution of just deserts as it has been applied to the sentencing of common offenders. Based on the writings of desert theorists, especially those of Andrew von Hirsch, the central tenets of desert are outlined. I then respond, in chapters 4 and 5, to the charges that desert is inapplicable in the context of corporate crime.

While most corporate-punishment theorists have largely ignored desert principles in their writings, those examining desert have focused much of their attention on its application to the punishment of what, for lack of a better term, are known as common offenses. Desert concepts came to the forefront of sentencing with the work of John Kleinig, and were made prevalent as issues meriting attention in sentencing by such scholars as Andrew von Hirsch, Richard Singer, and Joel Feinberg.

What desert theorists have not yet examined in any systematic fashion are the issues that surround the application of desert principles to the punishment of corporate offenders. Two concerns are paramount in this endeavor. First, the nature of corporate crime has unique implications in the assessment of seriousness of crimes—in particular, determining the harm and culpability of corporate offenses. The second issue involves the type and length of sentences applicable to corporations and individual agents.

Often, illegal acts in which corporations and their agents engage take place over a long period and present problems in determining the individual or aggregate injury produced. There are other types of corporate crimes in which the injury sustained may be relatively minor at the level of the individual victim, but great when viewed in terms of the total injury produced. This is often the case with price-fixing schemes, where a particular industry may reap millions of dollars as a result of collusion but where the individual (for example, the citizen who must pay an additional three cents per roll of tissue paper) suffers no substantial harm from the offense. Keeping in mind the nature of corporate crimes—the degree of injuries produced, the identification of victimization, and the variety of interests affected by the harm—how is it possible to rate the seriousness of the different offenses in a fashion that allows a meaningful gradation for the purposes of punishment?

Chapter 6 examines the general issues surrounding the assessment of harm of corporate offenses. In particular, I address the topics of corporate harm and the ranking of interests. In doing so, I incorporate and expand on a model of interest scaling first suggested by Joel Feinberg and adopted by Andrew von Hirsch. The model is developed with regard to the ranking of welfare interests and then applied and discussed in terms of scaling corporate offense seriousness.

Harm is only one component of seriousness, however. The issues entailed in determining culpability in the corporate context must also be examined. In chapter 7 I explore the culpability factors that may be considered in assessing blame for both corporations and individual agents. I review current theory on corporate criminal liability in the substantive context and note the implications of these (largely deterrent-oriented) theories with respect to the role of culpability in sentencing from a desert perspective. Drawing on the work of Peter French and the concept of corporate internal decision structures, I then examine the means by which culpability may be determined in the corporate context. The central tenet explored is that blame may be attached to the corporation as an entity when the illegal act by the corporation can be traced through a formal or informal organizational structure representing the decision-making channels, or the procedural rules and/or operating policy, of the corporation. This idea is expanded to the sentencing process, where I argue that the degree to which the criminal act is represented in the corporation's internal decision structure may serve as an indicator of the degree of blameworthiness for that act.

The issues surrounding the culpability of individual agents are then examined. Interesting dilemmas emerge with respect to the degree to which one may be considered blameworthy in the organizational context, particularly with respect to holding certain individuals responsible for specific intent offenses. Having examined these areas of concern, the analysis of the seriousness of corporate offenses concludes with a discussion of possible aggravating and mitigating circumstances and the use of prior record for corporate offenses, and how they may, or may not, be applicable.

The final topic concerns the scaling of punishments for corporations and their agents. The issues of ordinal and cardinal proportionality are reviewed in some detail and guidelines are offered. Current and proposed sanctions against corporations and individuals are then critiqued in terms of their accordance with desert principles. The use of the monetary fine (which appears to be one of the few sanctions applicable from a desert perspective) is then examined for corporations, paying particular attention to the day-fine system now used in Scandinavia and the United Kingdom.

The book concludes by reviewing the major components of a desert-based system of corporate punishment and outlines several of the practical concerns that are likely to confront efforts to develop such an approach.

Acknowledgments

THE ORIGINS of this book stem from my graduate training at the School of Criminal Justice, Rutgers University, and particularly from the education I received as a student of Andrew von Hirsch and Dick Sparks. Having studied with Andrew, I was swayed to the importance of desert in sentencing. From Dick, I learned something about both white-collar crime and the mysterious workings of the criminal law. It quickly became evident to me that those interested in desert had yet to address the complexities that arise with white-collar criminals, in particular those white-collar criminals who exist in organizational rather than in human form. At the same time, those interested in white-collar and corporate crime had spilled a considerable amount of ink on the role and importance of deterrence in sentencing but had largely ignored the role of desert.

A number of people merit acknowledgment for the thoughts that have tried to find a home in these pages. Obviously, Andrew von Hirsch tops the list. He has a gift, if that is the word I want, for finding the weak point in any argument, and his continual questioning and criticism—in the positive sense of that term—has made this a better book. Perhaps more than any other quality I admire his willingness to rethink and modify his own ideas. He serves as an excellent model for those interested in the pursuit of wisdom rather than mere truth.

Richard Sparks passed away in the summer of 1988, much to my and many others' sorrow. He cared deeply about his stu-

Acknowledgments

dents, and those who had a chance to benefit from his insights were truly privileged. He offered many important comments on earlier versions of this book, and I am indebted to him for his time as a mentor and for his friendship.

I would also like to thank Harold Pepinsky, with whom I work and have become close friends. He does not agree with most of what I have written, and his thoughts have been important considerations for me. Alas, he understands that change takes time. I would also like to thank John Braithwaite, Frank Cullen, Brent Fisse, Vagn Greve, Nils Jareborg, Paul Jesilow, Diane Vaughan, and David Weisburd for their helpful comments on all or portions of the manuscript. Thanks also to Chris Stone, who encouraged me to pursue this work.

I am also grateful to Northeastern University Press, and especially to Andrew Mandel, for their support and encouragement of this book. I would also like to thank Gina Doglione for her assistance, and patience, in typing the manuscript.

Most important, thanks to my family, immediate and extended, for their support during this work. Special thanks goes to Karen, Paul and Corey, who were the most supportive of all.

Finally, a version of chapter 4 appeared as "Desert, Retribution, and Corporate Criminality" in *Justice Quarterly* 5 (1988): 615–34.

Just Deserts for Corporate Criminals

CHAPTER 1

Punishing Corporations: From Practice to Theory

T HE TERM "white-collar crime," coined by sociologist Edwin Sutherland in 1939, was intended to distinguish illegal activity that occurs in relation to business from the activity that is normally considered crime (burglary, robbery, and the like).[1] Since that time, and largely as the result of Sutherland's own vagueness about the term, the study of white-collar crime has been preoccupied with definitions.[2] One result of this conceptual struggle has been an effort to determine which forms of illegal behavior may safely be called white-collar crime, with special attention paid to the criminal acts of large corporations.

Much of this attention has been fostered by two factors. First, awareness has grown of the tremendous harm committed by large corporations that manufacture defective products, endanger the lives of employees, pollute the environment, engage in illegal trade practices, and bribe public officials. The heavy-electrical-equipment conspiracy of 1962, Three Mile Island, Love Canal, the Exxon oil spill off and on the coast of Alaska, and the E. F. Hutton case, to name only a few, highlight the extent to which large corporations can inflict heavy damage on society—damage not only to the health and well-being of citizens, but also damage to the environment and to political and economic systems.

Just Deserts for Corporate Criminals

The second reason for this special attention to corporate criminality stems from its unique character. Corporate activity, legal or illegal, involves great numbers of people and a variety of goals and objectives. It involves organizational behavior and a structural framework which brings meaning to that behavior. It is this element that distinguishes corporate crime from other forms of white-collar crime. As Marshal Clinard and his associates state: "[C]orporate crime is actually organizational crime that occurs in the context of complex and varied sets of structured relationships and interrelationships between boards of directors, executives and managers on the one hand and between parent corporations, corporate divisions and subsidiaries on the other."[3]

Corporate crime is particularly difficult to define given the diversity of violations that may be committed in the corporate context and the wide variety of punishment options available. Limiting corporate crime to acts forbidden only in the criminal law can be too restrictive, since the majority of both minor and serious transgressions are relegated, as a matter of course, to civil and administrative remedies.[4] This presents particularly difficult problems in any attempt to gauge the amount of illegal corporate activity. Acts that merit the label "crime," in other words, acts that violate the criminal law, are not included because they are, for a variety of reasons, handled through the civil or administrative process. Unfortunately, if one chooses to include administrative and civil violations as part of corporate crime, as Clinard and Yeager have done, one risks being too broad.[5] Some illegal behaviors, such as reporting violations, get included as part of corporate crime and certainly act to distort our conceptions of the seriousness and extent of illegal corporate behavior. While a practical application of desert to corporate violations will ultimately require a sentencing body to consider which acts deserve criminal punishment and which do not, such an effort is beyond the scope of this study. For the purposes intended here, corporate crime will be considered as any act that violates the criminal law.

THE EVOLUTION OF CORPORATE
CRIMINAL LIABILITY

The outstanding feature of modern corporate criminal law is its lack of any consistent theoretical foundation. The development of corporate criminal liability has been piecemeal, drawing from the civil law and from individual criminal law. As a consequence, scholars continue to debate the appropriateness and structure of criminal liability for the corporate entity.[6]

In 1765, Sir William Blackstone wrote, "a corporation cannot commit treason, or felony, or other crimes, in its corporate capacity; though its members may in their distinct individual capacities."[7] This doctrine of *ultra vires* prevailed in the United Kingdom and the United States throughout much of the nineteenth century. However, as corporations expanded beyond the traditional public forms of cities, boroughs, and towns, and began to develop in both size and impact on the community, the courts soon found it necessary to address the question of criminal liability for the corporate entity. The first rulings addressing this concern in the United States followed much the same pattern as courts in the United Kingdom: corporations could be held liable for offenses of nonfeasance, but the courts hesitated to impose criminal liability for acts of misfeasance, which were generally understood to be affirmative acts.[8] It was not until 1854 in *State v. Morris and Essex Railroad Co.* and *Commonwealth v. Proprietors of New Bedford Bridge* that the courts extended corporate criminal liability to include misfeasance, arguing essentially that no great purpose was served in attempting to distinguish the doing of an unlawful act from the doing of a lawful act in an improper manner.[9] Although the attachment of criminal liability to instances of nonfeasance and misfeasance firmly established corporations as individuals in the eyes of the criminal law, no attempt was made until the twentieth century to impose criminal liability on corporations for crimes involving specific intent.

In 1909, the Supreme Court ruled that "there was no valid reason why corporations should not be found responsible for and charged with the knowledge and purpose of their agents."[10] Following this logic, the courts have, over the years, imputed to the corporation not only the acts of its officers (those who formulate corporate policy and run the corporation) and its middle managers (those who are involved, to a lesser capacity, in the decision-making processes of the corporation), but also the acts of lower-level "subordinate" employees who carry out the policies of the officers and middle managers. Following the civil-law doctrine of *respondeat superior,*[11] the acts of agents may be imputed to the corporation if:

1. The agent does, in fact, commit the crime. (Here, the courts have ruled that because the corporation consists of an aggregate of officers, middle managers, and subordinate employees, it is only necessary to establish that *some* agent, rather than a specific agent, committed the illegal act.)[12]
2. The agent commits the crime within the scope of employment. (Similarly, the courts have also come to regard the scope of employment to mean only that the act occurred in a job-related capacity.)[13]
3. The agent commits the crime with the intent to benefit the corporation.[14]

Punishing Corporations

Since the *Hudson River Railroad* decision of 1909, U.S. corporations have been held criminally liable for strict-liability offenses (those that do not require proof of criminal intent) and for offenses that require *mens rea*. Regulatory offenses generally consist of a failure to observe the statutory mandate, thus creating a risk of harm to the public. Because of the severity of the risk involved in several of these regulatory areas (for example, with the Food, Drug, and Cosmetic Act), efforts have been made by regulators to promote an "extraordinary standard of care." As a result, several of these regulatory offenses do not require proof of criminal intent.[15] However, while such strict liability offenses have been recognized as constitutional by the Supreme Court, they have fallen into disfavor in recent years. Legislatures now generally impose an intent requirement on most regulatory offenses.[16] Similarly, where no intent requirement has been established by the legislature, the courts have generally inferred such a requirement.

INDIVIDUAL LIABILITY IN THE CORPORATE CONTEXT

Within the corporate context, individual liability exists for direct actors (the individuals who physically commit the act) and for indirect actors (who may command or authorize the criminal act). The degree of intent necessary to establish criminal liability ranges from knowledge or willfulness,[17] to recklessness or negligence,[18] to strict liability. Most regulatory statutes establish intent directly. Where no intent requirements have been set forth, as in the Sherman Act, the courts have generally followed the ruling in *United States v. United States Gypsum Co.*, where it was determined that the conduct must be willful before criminal punishment can be imposed.[19] The standard of intent for principals (indirect actors) is sometimes spelled out

7

in the governing statute. If not, this standard is usually determined on the basis of the intent requirement establishing liability for the direct actor.[20] This has presented some problems, however, since the actions of the direct actor and the actions of those who authorize the activity are quite different. Neither the courts nor Congress have made much attempt to specify the conduct of indirect actors that is sufficient to prove intent.[21] As with corporate liability in general, there is considerable debate now going on regarding the standards to be used.[22]

THE ENFORCEMENT RESPONSE

When a corporation breaks the law, the enforcement actions available to government range from criminal proceedings to civil and administrative actions. The options available and the lack of any systematic procedure by which recourse is determined have made the study of corporate crime and punishment a frustrating endeavor.[23] As corporations grew in both size and impact on society, the government recognized a need to control the operations of these organizations more closely through the creation of special regulatory agencies. At first, these agencies were designed to deal with specific industries and were generally involved with such concerns as taxation, utility rates, transportation, interstate commerce, and banking.[24] However, as corporations began to markedly affect the health and safety of the public at large and the tremendous number of individuals in their employ, special regulatory agencies were formed specifically to protect society from harm. As a consequence, some three dozen federal agencies and "volume upon volume of regulatory laws have been created."[25]

From those agencies, Clinard and Yeager have identified twenty-four that maintain some enforcement responsibilities;

virtually all actions taken against a corporation originate in these regulatory bodies.[26] When a violation does occur, any of the following actions may be taken.

1. *Warnings.* The most lenient action available, a warning is a notice that a violation is occurring and that corrective action should be taken immediately.

2. *Recalls.* An administrative recall is generally imposed in violations involving highway safety, consumer-product safety, and food- and drug-related matters. Recalls may take a variety of forms, but are generally imposed after an official finding of a safety defect.[27] The offending corporation is then required to remove the product from the market until the defect is corrected.

3. *Unilateral Orders.* A unilateral order may be remedial and typically prescribes corrective actions to remedy the harm caused by the violation. Such orders may involve compensation to the victim, or they may mandate specific steps to be taken by the corporation to remedy the particular harm (for example, clean up pollution, reinstate employee(s)). A unilateral order may also take the form of a cease-and-desist command designed to prevent future harm. A cease-and-desist order may also require that affirmative steps be taken to ensure that the violation does not occur at a later date.[28]

4. *Consent Agreements.* A consent agreement entails an understanding between the offending corporation and the regulatory agency not to commit the violation again. This action differs from a consent decree in that the latter is ratified by the court. The consent agreement is the action most widely taken against corporations, since it entails neither prolonged investigation nor resource depletion to accomplish the specific deterrence intended. It is also

considered a valuable tool in that it allows the government to intervene directly in the operations of the corporation through such measures as the establishment of independent auditors or the appointment of outside directors, who would then make suggestions to the corporation regarding structural and operational changes necessary to prevent future violations. Similarly, consent agreements are acceptable to corporations because they allow them to escape criminal liability for an offense, thus reducing the likelihood that third-party damage suits will be filed against them for their violation.

·· 5. *Injunctions.* These are orders issued from the court calling for an immediate halt to the activity under scrutiny. Injunctions are most often used in cases of environmental pollution, trade violations, and product safety, especially when there is an urgent need to stop the activity until further investigations can take place.

·· 6. *Monetary Fines.* Such a penalty may be issued in either criminal or civil cases and represents the most common of the severe sanctions levied against corporations. As noted earlier, since the early twentieth century corporations have been held criminally liable for crimes requiring intent. For the most part, administrative remedies with an occasional civil fine until recently represented the normal course of action against corporate law violators. Today, with increasing pressure to impose both civil and criminal sanctions more often and more severely against corporations and their agents, most corporate criminal statutes not only authorize criminal fines but provide for a system of civil enforcement (including monetary penalties).

The decision to impose criminal or civil sanctions on a corporation for regulatory offenses is a difficult one, largely because there is no meaningful distinction in severity between a criminal fine and a civil penalty.[29] While there is a theoretical difference between the two sanctions, in that tort actions are intended to deter and compensate for damages and criminal sanctions are intended to punish and deter, this distinction has been blurred in practical application.[30] Civil fines may be calculated in terms of the damages caused by the act, but they may also include punitive damages, which represent some deterrent aim. Criminal monetary sanctions, on the other hand, have been characteristically low and seldom exceed the amount obtainable through civil remedies. The deterrent effect of the criminal conviction notwithstanding, there is often little difference between the two sanctions.[31] As a consequence, it is not uncommon for similar offenses that call for similar sanctions to be processed differently—one through civil court, the other through criminal court.[32]

Because both civil and criminal sanctions are available in most regulatory offenses, and because the distinction between the two remedies is often vague, those making the decision to prosecute have considerable discretion in choosing which route to pursue.[33] Once an agency discovers that a violation has occurred, it must decide first whether to prosecute the case at all. If it decides to proceed criminally, the agency must refer the matter to the Justice Department for prosecution. If the civil route is selected, the agency may refer the matter to the Civil Division of the Justice Department, or it may choose to proceed on its own with in-house attorneys.

Although there are criteria guiding the choice of which route to pursue, the factors used have not been clearly defined and therefore are left open to considerable subjective evaluation. Through interviews with agency personnel, Clinard and Yeager have derived the following factors considered relevant to the decision to proceed criminally or civilly: (1) the degree of •

loss to the public, (2) the level of complicity by high corporate managers, (3) the duration of the violation, (4) the frequency of the violation by the corporation, (5) evidence of intent to violate, (6) evidence of extortion, as in bribery cases, (7) the degree of notoriety engendered by the media, (8) precedent of law, (9) the history of serious violations by the corporation, (10) deterrence potential, and (11) the degree of cooperation by the corporation.[34]

In addition to their vagueness, these criteria vary substantially from agency to agency. Sam D. Fine, for instance, found that the standards used by the Food and Drug Administration included only the following: (1) the seriousness of the violation, (2) evidence of knowledge or intent, (3) the probability of effecting future compliance by the firm in question, as well as by others similarly situated as a result of the present action, (4) the resources available to conduct the investigations necessary to consummate the case successfully, and (5) the extent to which the action will benefit consumers in terms of preventing recurrences of the violation throughout the industry.[35]

Undoubtedly, the fourth factor mentioned by Fine, available resources, plays a large role in determining whether to pursue civil or criminal remedies. The very nature of corporate crime places great constraints on the enforcement capabilities of the regulatory agencies and the Justice Department. Often it is difficult to determine the exact nature of the crime, the harm that occurred or was risked as a result, and the individuals who participated. Determining these factors demands considerable manpower, technical knowledge, investigative capabilities, and time. Regulatory agencies, however, often lack sufficient finances and personnel to meet these demands.[36] Furthermore, these problems are compounded by mounting political pressure from industries against increased government regulation, by the political philosophy of the administration in power, and by a lack of agency coordination and communication.

Given these difficulties, and in light of the fact that the deterrent impact of civil sanctions roughly equals that of criminal sanctions yet is easier to obtain, the civil remedy has generally been the most widely pursued course of action.[37] Yet, this appears to be changing somewhat in recent years. Not only has there been a greater use of the criminal sanction for corporations and agents acting on their behalf, but the type and severity of the punishments have increased as well.[38] This response reflects a growing concern about corporate crime and the impact of corporations' wrongdoings on society, as well as a renewed interest by criminologists and legal theorists in the design and purpose of the corporate criminal sanction.[39]

THE RATIONALE FOR CORPORATE CRIMINAL SANCTIONS

While the imposition of criminal punishments for common crimes is normally thought of in terms of the combined purposes of deterrence, retribution, incapacitation, and rehabilitation, deterrence has generally justified the imposition of criminal sanctions for corporate misconduct.[40]

Incapacitation, which involves removing the offender from society or placing constraints on him so as to prevent him from committing criminal acts in the future, has generally not been considered a legitimate justification for the imposition of criminal penalties for corporate offenses.[41] This is largely because corporations, or individuals engaging in illegal behavior, are not believed to pose such a continued and dangerous threat to society as to merit incapacitation or imprisonment. One variant of incapacitation, selective incapacitation, calls for the • • identification of particular attributes of the offender or the of-

13

fense that point to continued criminal conduct. This task has proven difficult with common criminals, and there is by no means enough understanding of the activities of corporations or the behavior of individuals acting within corporations to begin to predict future corporate criminal behavior.

Yet, in recent years there has been a call to impose certain forms of punishment on corporations that, whether intentionally or unintentionally, include certain incapacitative effects. Christopher Stone, for example, has recommended suspending corporate officials from practicing their trade for three years.[42] These punishments, however, are not suggested as a response to protect the public from continued harm in specific cases, but rather as a response to the seeming incapability of existing punishments to adequately deter corporate crime generally.[43]

Until recently, rehabilitation has not been considered a legitimate justification for the imposition of corporate criminal sanctions. The purpose of rehabilitation—to alter an offender's "character, habits, or behavior patterns so as to diminish his criminal propensities"[44]—has not been regarded as an important need with corporate criminals, largely because there appears to be little about their behavior that the state can alter through treatment.[45] In addition, the nature of corporate crime is such that the isolated behaviors of single individuals are of secondary concern. Of more concern is the behavior of the group as a whole, a phenomenon about which little is known.

Lately, more attention has been paid to the idea of intervening directly in the structure and operation of the corporation itself.[46] Judicial intervention is not a new concept. In the past decade, several attempts have been made to intervene directly in the structure and operation of the corporation through civil injunctions and consent decrees. However, the

14

limited nature of consent orders has led a number of commentators to argue for the imposition of criminal sanctions designed to achieve the same end.[47] Such sanctions would allow for considerable intervention in the corporation without requiring consent from the corporation itself. Several courts have attempted such remedies, usually through corporate probation, but as yet little is known about the effectiveness of these interventions. Depending on the outcome of these efforts and the publicity they receive, the goal of corporate rehabilitation may well become a more frequently cited justification for the imposition of certain corporate criminal penalties.

Another rationale that justifies punishment is retribution. While the concept of retribution has received some attention in the literature on corporate punishment, the different interpretations of the term have led to confusion regarding its role in the substantive criminal law and in the punishment process. The confusion that surrounds the notion of deserved punishment will be discussed in greater detail later, but determining the role of moral blame in the context of corporate punishment has been a difficult task for those who practice and who write about corporate punishment.[48]

General deterrence refers to "the effect that a threat to punish has in inducing people to refrain from criminal conduct."[49] While there is little doubt that punishment does have some deterrent impact, there is considerable debate about how much deterrence takes place. Although many factors account for the extent of deterrence afforded by any given sanction, the responsiveness of the threatened population is particularly important.[50] Consequently, commentators have maintained that the nature of corporate crime is such that those engaging in it are particularly responsive to the threat of criminal sanctions. The most widely cited argument is that corporate crim-

15

inals, whether acting individually (in the name of the corporation) or as a collective body, base their actions on calculation rather than impulse. As William Chambliss has noted, the crimes committed by corporations are instrumental rather than expressive.[51] Unlike common criminals, whose actions may be the product of irrational processes not readily subject to control by the state, corporate criminals more often than not intend to achieve some specific and quantifiable profit-related aim, and they are generally regarded as rational individuals who act from a cost-benefit perspective.[52]

Another reason for the use of criminal sanctions in the corporate context is that corporate officials are normally concerned with minimizing risk in both their business and personal lives and are thus "risk averters" when confronted with the threat of punishment for their actions.[53] Because such individuals are thought to be much more future oriented than are common criminals, they are less willing to engage in activity that poses even minimal threats to the future of the corporation or to their own position within it.

A third reason for criminal sanctions is that corporations, and individuals acting on their behalf, tend to be particularly vulnerable to sanctions that threaten their financial or social status.[54] According to this argument, corporate officials, unlike most common offenders, are very much concerned about their standing in the community and the standing of the corporation in the business world. Corporate officials are generally considered to be pillars of the community, living in the most exclusive sections of town, belonging to the most prestigious clubs and organizations, and educating their children in the finest schools. The threat of the stigma of a criminal conviction, the fear of imprisonment in hostile and vulnerable conditions, or the possibility of cash fines reducing their economic standing is likely to constrain the acts of corporate officials much

16

more than common criminals, who are generally thought to have much less to lose.

Finally, Chambliss has identified one other reason why deterrent sanctions appear to work well against corporate criminals. Neither corporations nor the individuals acting on behalf of the corporation have a commitment to crime as a way of life.[55] The decision to commit a crime is generally a response to a unique set of pressures and not part of the usual pattern of business. Because crime is more often than not a singular response to certain contingencies, and because these individuals will generally seek legal recourse for dealing with those contingencies before choosing criminal means, many hold that the threat of criminal punishment is likely to have a greater deterrent impact on corporate criminals than on those who turn to crime as a regular solution to their problems and who are more familiar with the likely response.

Yet, while deterrence is commonly accepted as the primary reason for imposing criminal sanctions on the corporation and on individuals acting on the corporation's behalf, there is little agreement as to the type and severity of punishment that best achieves that goal. It is to this problem that I now direct my attention.

CHAPTER 2

The Deterrent Effectiveness
of Corporate Criminal Sanctions

U NLIKE the empirical research now being conducted on the effectiveness of punishments for common crimes, studies of the effectiveness of corporate criminal punishments remain largely theoretical. To the extent that empirical proof does exist for the deterrent effectiveness of corporate criminal sanctions, most studies only suggest that some punishment deters better than none at all. [1] Little is known about the deterrent effectiveness of specific sanctions (a situation made more complicated with corporate punishment, given the civil remedies that are also available), or whether varying the intensity of the sanction actually reduces crime. What is clear is that there appears to be a substantial increase in the number of corporate crimes. It is also known that civil remedies (injunctions and fines) constitute more than 90 percent of all actions taken against corporate violators. [2] A review of the literature on corporate punishment reveals a virtual consensus calling for the increased use of criminal sanctions, as well as an ongoing theoretical debate as to the kind of criminal punishment that would be most effective in deterring corporate crime. This chapter examines the current debate over existing and proposed criminal sanctions for both individuals and corporations: incarceration, monetary and equity fines, structural intervention, community service, and adverse publicity.

Just Deserts for Corporate Criminals
INCARCERATION

Many corporate criminal statutes authorize prison terms ranging only from one to five years.[3] Such periods of confinement are widely regarded as insufficient deterrents. Robert Ogren, for example, has argued in favor of increasing the maximum term of confinement to ten years, on the grounds that the present penalties "fail dramatically to cover the aggravated situations which call for harsh penal sanctions."[4]

Other commentators have called for an increase in the use of incarceration for white-collar criminals because they are punished less severely than their blue-collar counterparts, even though the white-collar offenses are equally severe (or more so) in the harms they generate.[5] However, two recent studies on the sentencing of white-collar offenders suggest that this disparity in punishment may not be as great as originally believed. John Hagan, Ilene Nagel, and Celesta Albonetti compared the sentences of white-collar criminals (defined as persons with a college education who committed specific occupational offenses) with the sentences of less-educated individuals convicted of the same offenses. They also considered the sentences of those with lower education who committed non-white-collar crimes and the sentences of those with higher educations convicted of the same offenses. They found that in general, though white-collar offenders spent less time in prison, there was little difference in punishment severity by educational attainment when the total sentence (including probation and fines) was considered.[6] In another study, Stanton Wheeler, David Weisburd, and Nancy Bode examined sentences for white-collar offenses only and found that both the probability of going to jail and the severity of the term *increased* with an increase in the occupational status of the offender.[7]

Corporate Criminal Sanctions

While these studies move beyond theoretical debate about the sentencing of white-collar offenders, they suffer from certain methodological limitations. The most significant of these is the definitions of white-collar crime that have been used.[8] Given the way in which data on white-collar crime are recorded, distinguishing offenses that take place in the corporate context from those that are occupationally related, but do not involve a corporation, is difficult. The result is that the sentencing of "white-collar offenders" may be substantially different from the sentencing of corporate offenders. Finally, while these studies have provided some information on the question of sentencing, they are limited to the extent that they reveal little about the "siphoning-off effect" that often takes place with white-collar offenders in general and corporate offenders in particular.[9] While it may be true that those who make it to the sentencing stage receive similar or more severe punishments as a result of social status, it must be remembered that the majority of corporate offenses carrying criminal sanctions are dealt with through civil remedies. A significant portion of corporate offenses never reach criminal court, much less the sentencing stage, and are therefore substantially underrepresented in this category.

Much of the hesitancy in imposing incarcerative sanctions on corporate offenders stems from the belief that other less severe punishments (such as fines, community service, or restitution) are equally effective in deterring illegal behavior. As one judge explains:

> Now, if restitution can be made, I think there are many cases where no incarceration is called for. Now here is a man whom I sentenced for a violation of securities laws. He pleaded guilty. And he had participated in defrauding investors, and in paying under the table commissions to brokers for touting his particular stock. The amount that he made, as it turned out, was something less than the inves-

tors lost. He undertook to make full restitution to the investors so that they ended up not losing anything, even though it was more than he made out of the deal. And I suspended the imposition of sentence in this case and placed him on probation with the special condition that he make full restitution to the investors. That in effect punished him because he paid more than he took in, and it helped the investors and it had the same deterrent effect as a period of incarceration.[10]

THE FINE

This is the most common punishment imposed against the corporation and its agents. Its use is based on the belief that corporate criminal activity is essentially profit-motivated behavior that can best be deterred by "hitting at the pocketbook." The typical fine imposed in the past, however, has been exceedingly low, representing "little more than a licensing fee" to conduct illegal acts.[11] As a result, some commentators have called for the elimination of fines and the imposition of more severe sanctions, most often imprisonment, aimed primarily at the individuals within the corporation.[12]

Others, basing their arguments on elaborate econometric analysis, have advocated the use of more severe fines.[13] The principle underlying this "economic school" is the belief that a specific and a general deterrent point can be located for corporate crimes by roughly calculating the costs and benefits involved. All acts of corporations, legal or otherwise, represent rational choices designed to maximize corporate profits. The desired outcome of the activity is defined by dollar value. To the degree that illegal activities represent the pursuit of other possible objectives—power and prestige, for example—the assumption remains that such objectives are readily reducible to monetary terms. Given this belief, the essential characteristic of cash fines is that they produce a disincentive to engage in misconduct by (at least) offsetting the gains of illegal activity. However, the actual imposition of cash fines in the past rarely

22

approximated this calculation. The fine levied against the investment firm of E.F. Hutton in 1988 demonstrates the disequilibrium between the benefits from the offense and the costs of punishment. Hutton pleaded guilty to some two thousand counts of fraud stemming from an elaborate check-kiting scheme. It is believed that the scheme garnered anywhere from four to ten billion dollars for the company. The fine imposed on Hutton was $215 million.[14]

In response to this disequilibrium, many have advocated an increase in cash fines.[15] Economists, however, have suggested that deterring corporate misconduct is more complex than simply upping the cash ante. Increasing the fine in proportion to the gain derived from corporate offenses is insufficient, given that so few corporate offenders ever get caught and convicted. It is necessary, they argue, to introduce into the equation a "nondetection factor multiplier," which takes into account the likelihood of apprehension.[16] For example, an act that has been rationally calculated to result in a $500,000 gain, but that only carries with it a 10 percent likelihood of apprehension, would require a punishment of $5 million to reach the minimal level of deterrence possible. This is said to be the minimal level because such a penalty only reduces the likely gains from the offense to zero. To ensure deterrence the penalty must create a negative expected gain and would therefore have to be in excess of $5 million.

William Breit and Kenneth Elzinga have argued further that deterrence requires one to consider whether the offender is a risk preferrer or a risk averter.[17] Attitudes toward risk alter the perceptions of disutility stemming from the probability of being caught. An enforcement strategy that reduces the likelihood of apprehension but increases the level of punishment if caught (it is assumed here that resource constraints force agencies to choose between increasing enforcement efforts and increasing the fines) will be attractive to a risk preferrer. Risk-averse offenders will prefer the strategy increasing apprehension for relatively small fines.

Given these propositions, effective deterrence requires some knowledge of the likelihood of being caught, as well as some knowledge of which corporations or individuals are prone to risk preference and which are prone to risk aversion. It is also assumed that corporate offenders are rational to the point of being able to render such calculations as they contemplate their future directions. Both these assumptions are untenable. While there can be little doubt that corporate actors are "reasoning" with regard to their offense, at least relative to other sorts of offenders, such a view of rationality seems overly optimistic. Recall the difficulty the various subcommittees and commissions investigating the so-called Iran-Contra affair had in determining the amount of money thought to be involved in the weapons-for-cash transactions and the confusion of even those directly involved. Similarly, while such a proposition seems plausible with offenses of an economic nature (price-fixing and the like), such crimes as bribery, pollution offenses, and occupational-health offenses are not so amenable to calculation. Seldom do bribes suggest a quid pro quo at set dollar amounts. Most bribes are provided as another form of advertising designed to direct specific clients toward certain services. Gains are to be expected, but amounts remain unknown.

Furthermore, while these economic propositions may be accurate in theory, they are unrealistic in practice, given the lack of information about the nature and incidence of corporate crime. Any attempt to calculate the likelihood of apprehension requires some knowledge of the "dark figure" of corporate crime—the vast amount of wrongdoing that goes undetected, or at least unacted upon. Further refinements would require such knowledge not only in the various categories of corporate criminality, but also in the various categories over time; one need only ask Ivan Boesky what he perceived the risks of apprehension for insider trading to be eight years ago relative to today.

A considerable amount of debate has revolved around the effectiveness of fines against the corporation versus fines against the individuals acting on the corporation's behalf. The imposition of monetary fines against the corporation for purposes of deterrence assumes that what drives a corporation is profit, pure and simple.[18] Yet, corporations are driven by other goals as well—including prestige, expansion, and compensation programs for executives. Consequently, focusing on short-term profit goals alone will miss the mark for many corporations.[19]

Although profit is likely to be a concern (albeit one of perhaps several), punishing a corporation by imposing a fine is assumed to achieve its deterrent aim in an indirect fashion by applying coercive force to the shareholders, officers and directors, and lower-level employees who make up the corporate entity.[20] Lowering corporate profits through criminal fines will have direct impact on the assets of shareholders and the incomes of upper- and lower-level employees. Put simply, corporate fines have deterrent impact by virtue of the fact that the goals of those punished indirectly (the officers and the employees) are the same as the goals of the corporation itself.

This assumption has itself been hotly debated. The most compelling argument against it has been made by Christopher Stone, who notes that, at least with regard to shareholders, "the absence of identity between the shareholder's interests and those of 'the corporation' is the very idea behind two of the basic notions of corporate and commercial activity: limited liability and bankruptcy."[21] Given this insulation, it is unlikely that shareholders are going to take the actions necessary to protect their interests, since their interests are not, in fact, threatened.

This insulation is also evident at the level of managers and directors, and on down to lower-level employees. Even assuming that managers and directors are profit motivated as well, the reality of corporate life is that "threats to the corporate treasury do not necessarily intimidate the top executives, whose tenure and salary almost inevitably survive lawsuits untouched."[22] Furthermore, managers and lower-level employees are likely to be motivated by the goals and objectives of the subunits in which they work, as opposed to the overall profit goals of the corporation. That the corporation is fined is not likely to have a consequence on the behavior of those at the lower levels unless the fine has a trickle-down impact on the subgoals of the individual units and departments within the corporation.[23]

In light of this predicament, one might assume that the best approach to deterring corporate crime would be to focus exclusively on the individual(s) responsible for the illegal behavior. Yet, this solution has been rejected by many, if not most, of the punishment theorists now writing about the problem. While it is often the case that corporate crime occurs at the lower levels of the corporate structure without the knowledge of those at the higher levels, it is also often true that the corporate hierarchy masks its own involvement by sacrificing those at the lower levels for carrying out its directives. Furthermore, upper-level management often exerts considerable pressure on lower-level employees to achieve goals with little regard for the means. Performance standards are established, but procedural criteria remain either unspecified or unclear. The employee quickly finds himself in a "damned if I do, damned if I don't" situation:

> Very large firms view middle-level managers as a fungible commodity that can be sacrificed as convenient scapegoats and easily replaced. Senior managers can piously express appropriate shock at their subordinates' actions while still demanding strict "accountability" on the part of such managers for short-term operating results.[24]

Fining the individual decision maker has also been criticized as an ineffective response simply because corporations can reimburse the employee for the fine and the expenses of the criminal action.[25] With the exception of the criminal stigma that may result from the conviction, the individual offender suffers no direct hardship from the punishment. Deterrence advocates argue that as long as corporations continue the policy of indemnification, few individuals will defy corporate directives calling (implicitly or explicitly) for illegal activity.

The alternative, once again, is to fine the corporate entity. Yet other criticisms arise with this approach besides the ones mentioned previously. Perhaps the most significant is that others not directly responsible for the illegal activity bear the burden of the punishment—shareholders, employees, and customers. It is often maintained that shareholders are the least affected by the injustices of fines. To a certain extent they did receive (or at least would have received) some tangible enrichment from the crime, thus creating some justification for their bearing a portion of the fine. Furthermore, all shareholders have the opportunity to pull out of the corporation with a minimum of harm at any point between the commission of the offense and the levying of the fine. That they maintain their holdings throughout an investigation, trial (should one take place), and sentencing demonstrates a willingness to risk their current holdings on the hope that no severe damage will result.

Yet, should shareholders bear the burden of the fine when they are arguably the least likely of those within the corporation to be aware that illegal activity was occurring?[26] Similarly, as noted by many corporate-punishment theorists, there is little reason to believe that modern corporate shareholders are in a position to direct the actions of the corporation in a way that realistically affects the mechanisms by which illegal conduct takes place.[27] To the extent that shareholders have any say whatsoever in the management of the corporation, that say tends to be restricted to the construction of broad policy objectives, generally of the long-term variety. Day to day decision making, the kind of decision making required to steer the corporation on a legal course, is outside the capabilities of shareholders who meet once or twice a year and who receive periodic updates through the mail.

This scenario also suggests that shareholders place high priority on law abeyance as a value seemingly independent of profitability. Yet, this form of *parens patria* cannot be assumed. With some rare exceptions, shareholders are not generally the functional equivalent of an errant child's parents. The interest in shareholders' corporate offspring is unifocused. As an advertisement for Phillips Petroleum once stated, "It's performance that counts." And performance here is measured by profitability alone. These errant children are merely abandoned and left wanting when they fail to live up to shareholders' expectations.

More important, the nature of corporate ownership has changed drastically over the past decades. Investing in corporations for long-term growth potential (the kinds of investments individuals are likely to make) has been replaced by investing for short-term, quick gains, exemplified most dramatically by the growth and development of program trading. Here, small changes dramatically affect ownership makeup within minutes, makeup that is largely composed of financial institutions and pension funds, controlling blocks of stock in the millions of shares. The bottom line is that these shareholders are concerned with the bottom line—short-term profit gains. To this extent, shareholders gauge the health of the corporation not with reference to specific management practices (for example, clear policy goals and unity of command), but instead with reference to financial trends and forecasts. While these trends may, in fact, be a product of effective (and legal) management and operations, they do not necessarily have to be. Financial trends and forecasts that predict short-term gains are influenced by many variables, often to the point where the relationship between profitability and good management may be spurious.

Shareholders notwithstanding, there are two other groups whose suffering as the result of fines is less easily dismissed. If the fine is serious enough to threaten the continued operation of the corporation, the company may reduce its impact by laying off employees or by reducing their benefits. Or, the corporation may pass on the cost of the fine to consumers, with the hope that those buying its products will fail to notice the increase or will not have the strength as a group to organize a collective response.[28]

Given the difficulty of determining the actual deterrent value of the fine, the ineffectiveness of focusing exclusively on the individual or the entity itself, and the external costs that often result from fines, most corporate-punishment theorists now advocate the use of a multitargeted punishment approach to deter corporate misconduct.[29] This strategy focuses on both the individual decision maker and the corporation itself and consists of a variety of relatively new corporate sanctions designed to overcome the inadequacy of fines.

THE EQUITY FINE

Perhaps the most elaborate of the new punishment sanctions now being suggested is the equity fine, proposed by professor John Coffee, Jr.[30] Equity fines are levied in equity securities of the corporation rather than in cash. According to Coffee, equity fines would allow for a punishment in excess of the liquid assets available to the corporation, thus allowing the fine to reach the necessary deterrence level. It would also reduce the spillover effect by focusing the fine on shareholders. Finally, because of its potential impact, more corporate control over managers would be likely to result, forcing misdirected managers' interests to align more closely with the larger concerns of the corporation.

Briefly, an equity fine would involve the same dollar value as that necessary to generate deterrence. However, the fine would consist of a block of new common stock in the corporation. These shares would then be issued to a state crime-victim-compensation fund or to some equivalent public-interest body. The fund would have the option of holding or liquidating its shares.

The equity fine overcomes the wealth-boundary of the corporation. The wealth-boundary problem, also termed the "deterrence trap," has been summarized as follows:

> The maximum meaningful fine that can be levied against any corporate offender is necessarily bounded by its wealth. Logically, a small corporation is no more threatened by a $5 million fine than by a $500,000 fine if both are beyond its ability to pay. In the case of an individual offender, this wealth ceiling on the deterrent threat of fines causes no serious problem because we can still deter by threat

of incarceration. But for the corporation, which has no body to incarcerate, this wealth boundary seems an absolute limit on the reach of deterrent threats directed at it.[31]

As Coffee notes, a cash fine is limited to the sum of the corporation's available liquid assets, plus its discounted market value as determined by future earnings. A corporation cannot, however, pay a fine based on future earnings unless it comes from equity securities:

> However, were we to impose equity fines, there is in principle no limit short of the total market value of the corporation. For example, if 1,000,000 shares are outstanding and were valued at $10,000,000 (i.e., $10 per share), we could impose a $9,000,000 fine by requiring the issuance of 9,000,000 shares.[32]

An equity fine is said to reduce spillover, since it does not affect either the corporation's liquid assets or its debt equity. Rather, the fine strikes shareholders only by "dividing the corporate pie into more and smaller pieces, thus reducing the price per share by the percentage of the stocks issued."[33] If, for example, the fine equals 10 percent of the common stock, price per share would drop 10 percent.

It is also assumed that the higher the equity fine, the greater the likelihood that shareholders will take corrective steps to monitor corporate activities. This would be realized through increased oversight of business decisions and through shareholder-derivative suits, which allow shareholders to pass on the cost of deterrence to responsible management, or, in the words of Coffee, "to those who are truly culpable."[34]

Coffee adds that further control over senior management may be achieved through fear of takeover attempts made opportune by the issuance of a large block of new shares. As the corporation becomes an attractive target for takeover, managers have good reason to fear for their continued employment. It is assumed that this fear would exceed the benefits that would accrue to the managers through illegal practices, even in instances where the same fears of job loss inspire managers toward illicit behavior in the first place. A further benefit is the possibility that the fine would represent a large enough block of stock to provide the victim-compensation fund with a seat on the company's board of directors. This influence would thus constitute a form of "public interest" often lacking in corporate governance.[35]

A final benefit suggested by Professor Coffee accrues with equity fines and serves to maximize general deterrence. Because stock prices reflect future earnings potential, corporations thought to be engaging in risky business would have diminished stock value.[36] Thus, the fine takes on something of a future-dangerousness rationale. Companies that have engaged in illegalities in the past, as well as companies that demonstrate dangerous characteristics (risky ventures and operational patterns) but have yet to be subject to sanction for them, would be viewed as highly suspect by investors. The stock market would then reflect this concern in the form of a lower price per share. This would, in turn, compel corporations to ensure that their behaviors are above reproach.

While the equity fine proffered by Professor Coffee is unique and offers creative ways around the problems of cash fines, it raises considerable problems in its own right. Most obvious is the difficulty associated with determining the value of the block of securities to be issued as punishment that will best achieve deterrence. Yet the equity fine has been criticized for other reasons as well.[37] For instance, doubts have been raised that equity fines would force the implementation of internal disciplinary programs or foster any incentive on the part of the corporation to remedy its problems.[38] Questions also arise about the effectiveness of the equity fine in aligning managers' interests, suggesting that managers will take steps to

32

minimize their potential financial loss or opt for nonstock compensation plans instead.

More important, the imposition of such fines raises serious questions of justice. Even though the equity fine promises to effect subtle and positive changes in the business operation there is simply no way to control its ultimate impact on the corporation. The last benefit suggested by Coffee exemplifies this point, as it raises concerns about the potentially punitive collateral consequences of stock market reactions to questionable conduct. Coffee himself notes that the deterrent effect achieved through share devaluation is in anticipation of wrongful conduct, often taking place prior to the crime.[39]

The disturbing implications of imposing punishment prior to the commission of an offense have, of course, been troubling ones with regard to individual offenders. Predictions of future dangerousness violate the fundamental retributive principle of punishment distribution—that offenders merit punishment only after having been found guilty of the act, and even then only with reference to the instant offense. It is true that sentencing practices violate this principle with regularity, considering such factors as offender characteristics typically associated with repeat offenders. Yet, the extent to which even this likelihood of dangerousness is considered is generally restricted to after the commission of the offense. That individuals should suffer from the stigmatization of the criminal process and the label attached to those found liable to punishment prior to the offense is untenable to those who value justice. Yet, this is precisely the result suggested, encouragingly, by Professor Coffee. Corporations that legally operate in risky activity or in an industry rampant with illegal activity (for example, those involved in the waste-disposal industry) would be subject to a de facto punishment through diminished share value brought on by the existence of a punishment system designed to bring such stigma about. This would be somewhat analogous to the disparagement brought on by being born black, where the stigmatization arises in recognition of the supposed relationship to crime and race and is documented by the disproportionality of black offenders involved in serious crimes. Those concerned with justice in punishment (as a generic issue, not simply as it relates to different kinds of offenders) would rebel against such reactions for a host of reasons not limited to concerns about the accuracy of the data or the extremely high likelihood of false positives. The same concerns apply here to corporate punishment. While one may argue that corporations do not suffer *in kind* as do individual offenders, corporations would, in fact, suffer unjustly. The concern here comes from what criminal punishment is said to represent *in principle* and the corruption of those principles by reacting in this fashion. While there is no doubt that equity fines allow for the imposition of severe financial penalties that might not be possible under a cash-fine system, given the significant problems associated with such a punishment, it is highly doubtful that the equity fine would ever be implemented as it is now designed.

STRUCTURAL INTERVENTION

Recent attempts have been made through civil injunctions to force corporations convicted of violations to remedy the internal processes that led to illegal conduct.[40] While some success has been reported, such injunctions are limited in their deterrent effectiveness. While an injunction may recommend that certain changes in the organization be made, the regulatory (as opposed to the punitive) nature of the remedy restricts the degree of intrusion and the ability to coerce the corporation into complying. For all intents and purposes, the reforms that are ultimately negotiated are those suggested and approved by the corporation itself. In some cases this has produced tangible results, but critics maintain that corporations are far less willing to take steps to reform their internal processes when those steps substantially alter the structure or operations of the company.

In response to the inherent problems of injunctions, recommendations have been made for structural intervention through corporate probation.[41] Proponents of this approach argue that it is both more efficient and effective than the use of fines. First, the reforms implemented by the court may be set at any cost level, so long as it does not exceed the minimum fine allowable. Second, by rectifying internal problems that lead to corporate violations, the likelihood of future violations by the same corporation is minimized. Third, corporate probation affords a degree of specific deterrence at the individual level, in that managers consider any outside intervention as a threat to their autonomy. Finally, probation is considered more efficient and just than fines, in that the problem of spillover is reduced.[42]

Corporate probation requires that offenders comply with specific conditions for a specific period.[43] The focus of the conditions is on modifying those features of the corporate organization that facilitate the commission of the offense. Advocates of corporate probation argue that the conditions must be designed to do any (or all) of the following: (1) evaluate and report data potentially relevant to the discovery or the prevention of future violations, (2) explicitly delineate the responsibilities of particular officials in response to that information, and (3) alter the organization's structure and/or process in such a way as to facilitate communication and responsibility regarding the decision-making function.[44]

Structural intervention is viewed as a rehabilitative device intended to alter the behavior of the corporation. Yet, such a sanction warrants concern, given the lack of knowledge about the causes of corporate crime. There is little empirical evidence available now to suggest that changes in the structure, communication systems, or operating procedures will, in fact, prevent corporate misconduct from recurring.

In light of what is known about corporate behavior from organizational theory, success in implementing policies would be difficult even if substantive evidence regarding the causes and solutions of corporate crime were available. Successful implementation often requires that changes be made in the corporation's missions, goals, power structure, tasks, and autonomy. In addition, changes may also be required in the external forces that act on the corporation. What makes changes in these areas so difficult for a rehabilitative perspective is that they are viewed with respect to one aspect of the corporation's life—its relationship to the law. In reality, however, the corporation is confronted with many other elements and is structured and operates in such a manner as to effectively deal with all of them.[45] The fact of corporate life is that the criminal law plays a minor role in its day-to-day operations. Primary concerns lie with production, sales, mergers, acquisitions, competition, and shareholder interests. A corporation's mission activates an ethos that is best suited to balance these various interests. Similarly, the structure and the tasks of the corporation are designed around these elements. While minor reforms (such as the appointment of an auditing committee to review safety data) will generally have little effect on the rest of the corporation's operations, any major reform that alters its structure and operations will have great impact on the rest of the corporation's activities and will, given the role the law plays in the life of the corporation, be fought every step of the way.[46] In this regard, conditions placed on corporations may be shortsighted and do more harm than good. As a dynamic entity, the corporation functions in a manner that goes far beyond merely complying with the law. Unless those implementing the reforms have some concept of how the corporation operates as a business entity, successful implementation may be impossible.

COMMUNITY SERVICE

Another rather new sanction directed at the corporation is the requirement that the corporate offender participate in some socially useful activity as a means of paying back society for the offense. This has been used quite often with individual offenders, largely because of reluctance to confine well-respected citizens and the inability of most of them to pay large fines.[47] The use of community service as a punishment for the corporation itself has received more attention in recent years, primarily because of the prevailing view that corporations ought to absorb the costs of their crimes and that the internalization ought to occur through some socially beneficial activity.[48] As Brent Fisse has noted, two concerns arise with the imposition of community-service orders on the corporation. The first is that judges will use the order to benefit some charity of their liking. The second is that corporations will cheat on the order. Fisse argues, however, that these concerns can be remedied by directing the community service to some area that is reasonably related to the offense for which the corporation was convicted and by appointing monitors to record the activities of the corporation as it complies with the community-service order.[49]

As with fines, the deterrent effectiveness of community service requires some form of cost-benefit analysis, and, as demonstrated above, this is no easy task. While imposing community service may create more deterrence than imposing no form of punishment at all, the issue that must be addressed is the amount of deterrence that is expected given the cost of the community service. Community service may be more attractive because of the social good that results, but the test is whether or not it leads to a reduction in crime. It is difficult to imagine that such a punishment will be any more effective than the sanctions now imposed in achieving this aim.

ADVERSE PUBLICITY

Fisse favors adverse publicity as the "quintessentially stigmatic corporate sanction."[50] Fines are directed only at the financial motivations of corporations. Yet corporations are also motivated by such nonfinancial goals as prestige and power. To achieve these ends, the corporation must present a good image to both the public and its competitors. In a study of the impact of adverse publicity on seventeen major corporations, Fisse and his Australian colleague John Braithwaite found that the loss of corporate prestige (as distinct from financial loss) was considered an important concern in all but two cases.[51] They argue that unlike individual criminal stigmatization, which may produce adverse psychological effects and drive the person further toward crime, stigmatization of the corporation is likely to produce a positive response that initiates changes in the corporation to protect its prestige.[52] Given the important role of prestige in a corporation's operations, the authors advocate the use of criminal sanctions designed to notify the public that the corporation has been convicted of a serious violation of the law. They recommend that publication of the details of the offense be part of a court-ordered sentence, and that presentence orders be used to require disclosure of organizational reforms taken as the result of the offense. Such publicity should also include the names of responsible persons and the disciplinary actions taken against them (thus creating a deterrent effect at the individual level as well).[53]

Several criticisms have been levied at the use of adverse publicity against corporations. One argument is that the corporation can simply engage in a counterpublicity campaign to offset the impact of the punishment, in much the same way that General Electric used Ronald Reagan to bolster its image after its conviction in the heavy-electrical conspiracy cases in 1962.[54]

The most significant criticism of the use of adverse publicity as a punishment is that it is very difficult to control. The impact of the punishment depends on the extent to which the public is willing to take steps to act against the corporation. The result is that there simply is no way to gauge the deterrent effect or severity of such a sanction.

CONCLUSION

The past decade has witnessed a call for the increased use of criminal sanctions to deter corporate misconduct. To date, the most commonly imposed criminal penalty is the fine. Yet, the use of criminal fines has been criticized on the grounds that their present level is too low to effectively discourage crime. Furthermore, the fines do nothing in and of themselves to remedy the problem. Rather, they leave any corrective measures in the hands of the corporation itself. In response to this problem, a number of corporate-punishment theorists have suggested that the entire corporate-sanctioning system be revamped. Recommendations include increasing the criminal fine, greater use of imprisonment, structural intervention, community service, and adverse publicity.

These dispositions are, of course, utilitarian in their intent. And, as demonstrated, the allocation of punishments is determined (at least theoretically) by utilitarian cost-benefit calculations. In its purest form, the severity of the punishment for any given offense would equal the average gain from the offense multiplied by some factor representing the average likelihood of apprehension for the offense. Although little has been written on the allocation of punishments that take the form of imprisonment, structural intervention, community service, or adverse publicity, it can be safely assumed that the cost-benefit equation holds true in those cases as well.

The cost-benefit calculations do not stop here, however. There will always be deviations from this average, and so some crime will continue. How much crime do we as a society tolerate? The utilitarian response is to weigh the costs, where costs are measured by the expenses imposed on both society and the offender, and the benefits, which derive from the reduction in crime. Neither of these calculations is easy. As we have seen, the problems in determining the average gain for an offense are superseded only by the problems in determining the risk of apprehension. And, while empirical studies continue to flourish, there is currently little substantive empirical evidence to suggest that varying the intensity of punishments leads to a reduction in crime. It is perhaps because of these difficulties that the current state of corporate punishment is in disarray; serious offenses often carry lenient sentences, and minor offenses often carry relatively harsh punishments. It is the rule more than the exception that offenders convicted of the same offense receive very different sentences, often going so far as to have more severe civil fines than criminal fines imposed for similar types of offenses. It is, at present, a sanctioning system without logic, characterized only by wide judicial discretion and tremendous disparity in punishment.

A little over a decade ago, a new body of sentencing literature emerged in reaction to similar conditions existing for the punishment of common criminals. The focus of the literature is on the concept of desert, rather than crime control, as the basis for the allocation of punishments. Let us now turn our attention to this theory.

CHAPTER 3

The Development of Desert

MODERN desert theory emerged in the early 1970s as a response to the inadequacies that prevailed in the existing sentencing system.[1] Since the late nineteenth century, American sentencing ideology has been influenced by the positivistic belief that criminal tendencies could be identified and cured. This emphasis on prediction and rehabilitation fostered the development of a wide variety of punishment options, the imposition of which was based on the offender's likelihood of returning to crime and his amenability to treatment.[2] In addition, the sentence length was indeterminate; those who demonstrated progress toward rehabilitation could be released earlier than those whose "cure" had yet to take effect, and those who demonstrated a continued risk to the community could be held until that risk was no longer prevalent. To achieve the desired goals, judicial and bureaucratic discretion was essential. Judges were given a wide range of sentences from which to tailor the appropriate "individual" penalty that best suited the offender at hand, and parole boards were given great leeway in deciding the ultimate stay of the offender once in confinement.

CALLS FOR REFORM

Skepticism toward the guiding positivist ideology in sentencing began to develop in the mid 1960s.[3] By the mid 1970s that skepticism had grown to intense criticism and calls for reform.[4]

Just Deserts for Corporate Criminals

Much of the criticism focused on the problems associated with prediction. Caleb Foote, writing for the American Friends Service Committee, called for the repeal of the indeterminate sentence on the basis that preventive detention, as opposed to rehabilitation and deterrence, served as the primary basis for imprisoning offenders, and that a number of offenders were being held in spite of the fact that they would not have committed another offense if released.[5]

The problem of overprediction has generated considerable research in the past decade, with the majority substantially confirming Foote's concern. Violent offenses are especially difficult to predict, given the rarity of their occurrence.[6] A review of clinical and actuarial attempts to forecast violent recidivism revealed that the rate of false positives (persons mistakenly predicted to return to violent crime) ranged from 60 to 99 percent.[7]

Criminologists have attempted to develop prediction instruments that reduce the number of false positives. While some success has been reported, statistical approaches are still confronted with relatively high incidences of this type of error.[8] Furthermore, they are rather limited in what they can predict. Prediction tables are static instruments. They are, at present, deficient in determining which offenders are likely to repeat, or in predicting the effectiveness of various types of punishments in reducing recidivism.[9]

The problem of prediction was not the only concern emerging in the mid 1970s. Sociologists, psychologists, and criminologists all began intensive evaluations of correctional rehabilitation programs, reaching a general consensus that the programs were generally ineffective in reducing recidivism.[10] The most widely cited study revealed that few of the two hundred correctional treatment programs evaluated showed evidence of success.[11] Although this examination has come under some criticism, other studies (including a review conducted by the National Academy of Sciences) have also questioned the effectiveness of past rehabilitative efforts.[12]

Recently, reports have been released indicating that particular programs might be effective given certain subpopulations of offenders identified as being in need of that specific type of treatment.[13] However, the present attitude toward a rehabilitation-focused punishment scheme, at least among most criminal justice experts, remains largely pessimistic.

The disparity inherent in the indeterminate and partially determinate sentencing system has also drawn increased criticism. Widely diverse sentences were imposed for offenders convicted of similar crimes.[14] This disparity was brought to light in a study commissioned by the judges of the U.S. Court of Appeals for the Second Circuit.[15] In that work, fifty federal judges were given twenty identical files (from actual cases) and asked to impose a sentence for each defendant. The result showed vast differences not only in the length of sentence provided, but in the type of sentence as well. Similar discrepancies were also found among the lengths of confinement recommended by parole boards.[16] Although other studies have found less deviation in sentencing patterns, the concern is not so much with the statistical norm of the results, but with the decision maker's freedom to deviate from the norm without providing reasons for that deviation.[17]

Perhaps the most troubling aspect of the positivistic ideology evident during this period was the general disregard for the notion of proportionality in punishment. Expectations as to the effectiveness of both rehabilitation and prediction in reducing crime allowed utilitarian premises to overshadow the concerns for equity and fairness in the treatment of offenders. Persons convicted of less serious crimes could be deprived of their liberty for long periods on the basis of their supposed

45

dangerousness or need for treatment. Similarly, offenders convicted of serious offenses could receive substantially less severe punishments (both in type and duration) if they were deemed "integratable" and/or treatable.[18] Furthermore, the lack of any formal guidelines for judges and parole boards governing the imposition and duration of sentences created a situation in which substantially similar offenders convicted of substantially similar offenses could be given very different punishments for no readily apparent reason.

In response to these problems, several proposals for reform began to emerge. In 1979, the American Bar Association's Task Force on Sentencing Alternatives and Procedures recommended the creation of sentencing standards designed to reduce much of the existing discretion afforded to judges and parole officers.[19] Rehabilitation was discredited entirely as a justification for the type and duration of punishments imposed. Although the concept of proportionality was delegated a more significant role in the determination of punishments, the severity of the sentence was to be based on the offender's likelihood of returning to crime. The seriousness of the offender's crime was to be considered only in terms of supplying boundaries to the utilitarian determinations. If the intensity of the punishment were overly disproportionate (in either direction) to the seriousness of the offense it would distort notions of blame.[20]

Questions as to the effectiveness of predictive techniques notwithstanding, the task force maintained the preeminence of selective incapacitation as a means of protecting the public from harm. According to the report, while fair treatment of offenders should be a factor in sentencing guidelines, the right of society to be free of harm from criminals outweighs the rights of individual offenders, and should therefore be the primary concern in sentencing decisions. Fairness for the offender could be guaranteed by imposing broad proportionality constraints and by eliminating criteria unrelated to criminal conduct (for example, race, education, and marriage) as the basis for predicting continued criminal behavior.[21]

The reforms outlined by the task force were not the only remedies suggested for dealing with the inadequacies of the postivist-based system of punishment. The "Chicago School," with its reliance on econometric models and its emphasis on deterrence and incapacitation, responded to the growing crime rate with the recommendation that mandatory minimum prison terms be imposed for those convicted of serious offenses.[22] According to this position, a more effective and efficient way of reducing crime is to ensure that serious offenders receive *some* time in jail.[23] The ultimate decision of how much to punish for any given offense would therefore be based on the reduction in crime (for any given category) that the punishment is expected to produce, versus the cost of confinement (or other sanction) and concerns for the pain inflicted on the offender.[24]

According to these deterrence advocates, the sentencing system should be structured to reduce sentencing discretion by judges and parole officers. The sentence should be based on cost-benefit calculations, and must remain consistent so as to produce the desired deterrent effect. Similarly, proportionality should be a consideration, not on the basis of issues of fairness, but because failure to keep punishments somewhat proportional to the seriousness of the offense would either entice offenders to commit more serious crimes or create an unwanted overdeterrence.[25]

THE EMERGENCE OF DESERT

While deterrence took center stage during the 1970s, a growing body of sentencing literature was emerging with a very different view of the purpose and distribution of punishment. Unlike the positivist sentencing rationale and the other reform models being proposed, with their central focus on utilitarian, crime-control concerns, this new literature emphasized the moral aspects of punishment and the fairness and equity issues that revolve around the punishment of individual human beings. Grounded in civil-libertarian concerns for individual rights, punishment is viewed from this perspective as "a solemn act of ascribing blame."[26] Punishment not only entails harsh treatment, but also condemns the actor for wrongdoing.[27] It is this condemnatory aspect that separates punishment from other types of penalties, most notably those imposed through civil actions.[28] While it is considered a general requirement of justice that those not responsible for their actions (and therefore not blameworthy) should not be condemned by the state, the degree of blameworthiness of an offender's conduct has generally not been considered in any systematic manner in the context of the sentencing process. Yet, not only does the criminal sanction itself imply blame, but the type and the severity of punishment reflect the degree of blame imposed on the offender.

Given the importance of the condemnatory feature of punishment, the allocation of punishment from a desert perspective is not based on some forward-looking aim. Its focus is on the wrongfulness of past conduct. The extent of punishment is therefore based on the seriousness of the offense,[29] as determined by two elements: the harm that took place or was risked by the act and the culpability of the actor. Harm refers to the injury that occurred from the act, or might have occurred had the act been carried to completion. Culpability refers to the intent of the actor, determined generally by the *mens rea* requirements that define the degree to which the offender is responsible for the act. Also included in the notion of culpability are such factors as motive, such excuses as necessity and duress, and such defenses as insanity. Even though the theory of commensurate deserts is relatively new, several states have incorporated its principles into their own sentencing guidelines in varying forms.[30]

THE CENTRAL TENETS OF DESERT

The term "just deserts" has come to mean many different things to different people. This confusion has hindered the development and application of the concept. Andrew von Hirsch has attempted to clarify the central features of desert by distinguishing three different levels of application.[31]

The first level concerns the relevance of desert principles to the justification for the existence of the criminal sanction. Here, the criminal sanction cannot be explained with reference to desert, or, more appropriately, reprobation, by itself; crime-control considerations also come into play. According to von Hirsch, "prevention explains why the state should impose material deprivations on the offenders. Reprobation for wrongdoing justifies why the deprivations should be visited in the condemnatory fashion that characterizes punishment."[32]

The second level of the theory concerns ordinal penalty gradations and involves the comparative severity of punishments.[33] Proportionality serves as the guide here, both in terms of parity (treating similar offenders the same) and rank of the various crimes. As Richard Singer has noted: "To punish an armed robber and a thief with the same punishment has two effects: (1.) it unfairly increases the amount of moral stigma and condemnation imposed upon the thief (assuming armed robbery is a more serious offense); and, (2.) it unfairly reduces the amount of moral stigma and condemnation imposed upon the armed robber."[34] Simply put, offenders who commit the same offense merit equal censure as expressed by the amount of punishment, and, as the seriousness of the offenses increases, the punishments should also increase proportionally in severity to reflect the increased reprobation merited by the acts. Offenders convicted of similar offenses may only be punished differently if other factors relating to harm and culpability aggravate or mitigate the seriousness of the offense. Even here, however, the degree to which the punishment increases or decreases should be minimal.

The third and final level of the theory relates to the "cardinal magnitude" of the punishment scale. This concerns the absolute maximum and minimum levels of punishment imposed and the "anchoring points," which reflect changes in the different types of punishments (for example, probation to incarceration). Desert provides no immediate solutions to these particular issues.[35] While it is possible to express a range of punishments that reflects what is and is not deserved, it is difficult, and to a large degree meaningless, to come up with a uniquely "deserved" punishment for offenses. Given this range of uncertainty, other concerns, some of which may focus on crime control, may come into consideration in determining these parameters.[36] What is crucial to understand, however, is that once the anchoring points have been established, the punishment scale must be graded in a fashion that reflects the comparative seriousness of the offenses. To rank the punishments within the scale on utilitarian grounds would violate the important principles of maintaining ordinal proportionality.[37]

The framework provided by von Hirsch clarifies the relevance of desert concerns to the different components of punishment. While the theory progresses, lingering questions remain. Exactly how is seriousness to be determined? What components enter into the assessment of harm and culpability and how are these two factors to be combined to determine seriousness? What considerations may be involved in the determination of the absolute levels of punishment and the anchoring points in the punishment scale? What factors may be considered in terms of aggravation and mitigation and how may they be entered into the construction of the punishment scale? Those currently writing on desert have provided initial insights into these questions. It is hoped that in examining the application of desert considerations to the punishment of corporations and their agents the theory will progress even further.

Desert, Retribution, and the Theory of Punishment for Corporations and Their Agents

P RINCIPLES of commensurate deserts maintain that punishments should be allocated on the basis of the seriousness of the offense and that like offenses should receive like punishments. Those writing on the application of criminal punishments to corporations and their agents have not considered the role of desert in any systematic fashion.[1] To the extent that desert has been considered, it has generally been dismissed as either inappropriate or not feasible in the context of corporate criminality. Two major arguments are often cited in support of this dismissal. First, retributive principles, in which desert is included, are not applicable as justifications for corporate criminal sanctions because such concepts as vengeance and restoring benefits and burdens make little sense in the realm of corporate activity.[2] Second, desert, which focuses on the importance of blame, seems inapplicable for regulatory offenses that are not considered morally wrong.[3] Both arguments are open to challenge. This chapter examines each of them in detail, and posits that retribution is an acceptable, though not necessarily independent, justification for corporate punishment and that desert

53

should serve as the principal means by which punishments are allocated for corporate criminality. The first part explores the variety of retributive theories of punishment, including revenge, Kantian benefits and burdens, and reprobation, and the extent to which principles of desert are applicable within each version. The second part examines the argument concerning the moral neutrality of corporate crime and the impact that such a stance has on the incorporation of desert criteria in corporate punishment. The chapter concludes that neither argument serves as a sufficient reason for the exclusion of desert principles in the punishment of corporations.

A review of the corporate-punishment literature reveals two areas of confusion about the role of desert in the punishment of corporations. First, while the concept of desert is generally employed in theories of retribution, the notion of retribution itself is a muddled one, particularly with reference to punishment.[4] Theories ranging from concepts of pure and simple revenge, to Kantian notions of restoring benefits and burdens, to more recent ideas that emphasize the reprobative value of punishment are all said to be retributive, but they differ in important respects. Clearly, substantial problems arise when punishment is justified in terms of "an eye for an eye," or even by vague notions of redistributing benefits and burdens. Because of the problems posed by some of these retributive explanations, the tendency has been to dismiss, in a summary fashion, *all* retributive justifications for punishment, including the concomitant principle of desert.

Second, much of confusion about retribution and desert can be understood through what H. L. A. Hart calls the interrelated features of punishment—the definition, the general justifying aim, and the distribution (the last concerning questions of liability and amount).[5] In response to a general drive to oversimplify the complex issues surrounding punishment, Hart states:

> What is needed most is not the simple admission that instead of a single value or aim (Deterrence, Retribution, Reform or any other) a plurality of different values and aims should be given as a conjunctive answer to some single question concerning the justification of punishment. What is needed most is the realization that different principles (each of which may in a sense be called a "justification") are relevant at different points in any morally acceptable account of punishment. What we should look for are answers to a number of different questions such as: what justifies the general practice of punishment? To whom may punishment be applied? How severely may we punish? [6]

The recent literature on just deserts concerns the distribution of punishment, particularly the question of amount. Desert theory does not specifically address the issues surrounding the general aim of sanctions, or the question of to whom punishment may apply. [7] Yet, it has been mistakenly assumed that for desert to be applicable as a justification for the amount of punishment it must also stand alone or serve as a primary justification for the existence of punishment. [8] This insistence, combined with the general confusion surrounding retributive notions in general, has led to a misunderstanding about the role of desert in the sentencing of corporations and agents acting in their behalf.

Two tasks must be undertaken to clarify this misunderstanding. The first is to examine and critique the retributive perspectives that appear in the corporate-punishment literature and to make meaningful distinctions between such terms as vengeance, retribution, and desert. The second is to identify the role desert plays at the different levels of punishment and to discuss how the levels relate to each other, if at all. It will become evident that the quick dismissal of desert principles is unmerited.

Just Deserts for Corporate Criminals
REVENGE, RETRIBUTION, AND DESERT:
DISTINCTIONS AND APPLICATION TO THE
GENERAL JUSTIFYING AIM OF PUNISHMENT

Punishment as Revenge

As with the general literature on punishment, the literature on corporate punishment varies widely in its use of the term "retribution." One tendency is to dismiss retribution outright as little more than simple revenge.[9] Revenge is indeed a retributive concept in the sense in which H. L. A. Hart speaks, whereby some value other than crime prevention is gained through the imposition of punishment.[10] In this interpretation, the value of the punishment lies not in the likelihood that the offender will cease his activities, but in the personal satisfaction that is gained by "settling the score."

Yet, most modern punishment theorists appear unwilling to accept revenge into the retributive fold. Revenge focuses principally on the response or "impulse" of the *victim* to lash out at the offender, whereas retribution focuses not on the victim, but rather on the offender's wrongdoing and the appropriate repayment *by society* for that wrongful behavior.[11] Furthermore, while retribution and revenge entail the idea of repayment, there is little in the concept of revenge to suggest the extent of the repayment necessary for vindication. Nothing prevents the punisher from inflicting injury to the offender severely disproportionate to the gravity of the offense.[12] Yet, a central concept of retribution that helps to set it apart from revenge is the principle of proportionality between offense and punishment.

Classical Retributive Theory:
Restoring Benefits and Burdens

Retributive theories "maintain that culpable conduct deserves

56

punishment, regardless of the considerations of social utility."[13] Most punishment literature has focused on the retributive rationale for punishment as first espoused by Kant, later by Hegel and Bradley, and more recently by John Finnis and Jeffrie Murphy.[14] Here the focus is on the classical notion of the restoration of benefits and burdens through punishment.

The premise of the benefits and burdens theory is that citizens of equal capacity and ability are bound together by a system of rules that maximizes individual freedoms. Compliance with these rules provides benefits to all. According to the Kantian view, in a system that maximizes individual freedom a person who chooses to violate the rules set down by society acts as a "free agent," recognizing that "his own evil deed draws the punishment upon himself."[15] Notice that the concept of desert is inherent in this notion. Desert entails a response to an individual, in this instance punishment, merited by virtue of some quality or act (wrongdoing) of that individual. Furthermore, when an offense has been committed, it is not simply permissible to punish, but the state is required to do so:

> Even if a civil society resolved to dissolve itself with the consent of all its members—as might be supposed in the case of a people inhabiting an island resolving to separate and scatter themselves throughout the whole world—the last murderer lying in prison ought to be executed before the resolution was carried out. This ought to be done in order that every one may realize the desert of his deeds, and that bloodguiltiness may not remain on the people; for otherwise they will all be regarded as participators in the murder as a public violation of justice.[16]

Central to this argument is that punishment is deserved by offenders because of the wrongfulness of their deeds, and that punishment is morally justified on grounds independent of utilitarian (crime-reduction) considerations. Kant is less clear, however, as to the purposes that punishment *does* serve.[17] One interpretation of his position is that the crime represents action that, if universalized, would destroy freedom. When the offender chooses to commit the act, he or she accepts that such behavior is universalizable. The act of punishment represents an extension of this belief and demonstrates to the offender the consequences of such universality. As K. G. Armstrong has stated, "[punishment] demonstrates to the offender the full gravity of what he has done."[18]

Hegel appears to agree that punishment serves to show the actor the wrongfulness of his actions and is therefore justified on those grounds. He expands, however, on the additional values that such punishment may foster. Crime represents an invasion of a right. To let the invasion of the right proceed without punishment is to give such action legitimacy. When offenders choose to commit a crime, they demonstrate that the burdens which protect their rights, as well as the rights of others, are not binding on them. Justice is then violated, since the system of justice demands that the rights of others be respected. Thus, among the functions of punishment, from the Hegelian perspective, are the restoration of the balance of justice through the exaction of a debt, and the reestablishment of the legitimacy of the system of benefits and burdens itself.[19]

Murphy's interpretation of Kant stresses the importance of reciprocity as a means of securing political obligation among those in society. According to Murphy, this "quasi-contractual model (also found in the writings of John Rawls[20]) states:

> In order to enjoy the benefits that a legal system makes possible, each man must be prepared to make an important sacrifice— namely, the sacrifice of obeying the law even when he does not desire to do so. Each man calls on others to do this, and it is only just or fair that he bear a comparable burden when his turn comes. Now, if the system is to remain just, it is important to guarantee that those who disobey will not thereby gain an unfair advantage over those who obey voluntarily. *Criminal punishment thus attempts to*

maintain the proper balance between benefit and obedience by ensuring that there is no profit in criminal wrongdoing.[21]

Some scholars have questioned the so-called nonutility of the benefits and burdens theory, suggesting that the desire to ensure no profit from criminal wrongdoing entails some consideration of social utility. According to these arguments, maintaining the balance of benefits and burdens prevents future chaos (and, logically, crime) that would stem from a growing sense of unfairness.[22] In response to these claims, Murphy points out that the failure to maintain reciprocity represents an *injustice* of the greatest sort, regardless of the consequences that may result from the failure to obey the rules. It is not the consequences, but the "injustice itself" that merits retribution. Crucial here is the distinction between those theories of punishment that disregard these moral convictions (justice) or view them simply as factors, frustration of which makes for socially undesirable excitement, and those theories (such as Kant's) that out of deference to those convictions themselves justify punishment.[23]

Finnis has criticized Murphy's account of retributive justice as too obscure, particularly with reference to the nature and occasion of the criminal's profiting from law-breaking behavior.[24] He suggests that the ambiguity can be clarified by viewing the offenders' gain in terms of the general "advantage of indulging a (wrongful) self-preference," not in terms of excessive freedom of choice that other law-abiding citizens voluntarily denied themselves. The advantage gained by the offender cannot be lost until the "criminal has the disadvantage of having his wayward will restricted in its freedom by being subjected to the representative 'will of society' (the 'will' which the offender disregarded in disregarding the law) through the process of punishment."[25] From this perspective, fairness has little to do with the material benefits derived by the crime, but instead focuses on the general disadvantage that results from choosing to stay within the confines of the law while others choose not to.

Like punishment theorists in general, those writing on corporate punishment have concentrated on the problems associated with the restoration of benefits and burdens. In general, the criticism has been directed at the idea of punishment as a vehicle by which the proper balance of benefits and burdens may be maintained, and the seemingly concomitant principle of *lex talionis:* that the means to restore this balance is by returning "like for like." Stephen Yoder states, for example, that "the desire for retribution is, after all, basically an emotion, and to have to quantify and apply so volatile a factor in a criminal sanction would be difficult indeed."[26] Braithwaite criticizes the concept of benefits and burdens in the corporate context because corporations differ considerably from individuals in the values they maintain. Retribution cannot suffice as a justification for the institution of corporate criminal sanctions since

> there can be no meaningful balancing between individuals and corporations because there is no commensurability between them with respect to the attributes at issue. It is nonsense to say of the punishment of corporations that "after having undergone punishment, the violator ceases to be at advantage over his non-violating fellows," where the latter are individuals.[27]

Braithwaite raises important concerns for the benefits and burdens theory. The idea that crime represents a clear and present "advantage," and that punishment affords a means by which that advantage may be discounted, is difficult to fathom, regardless of the offender's corporate or human constitution. As von Hirsch notes, "punishment, unlike compensation, does not in any literal sense restore the fair distribution of social benefits that the wrongful act has disrupted. This means that the benefits and burdens argument would have to be bolstered by a wholehearted social contract theory in order to be sustainable."[28]

The benefits and burdens position, particularly as held by Finnis, has also been challenged on the grounds that it relies too heavily on the belief that the social system and its distribution of benefits is fair to begin with. Conflict theorists in particular are quick to point out that the economic and political systems, and the arrangements that derive from them, are seldom fair toward all.[29] An institution of punishment built on such a premise becomes untenable when the reciprocal benefits of the law serve only a decidedly small segment of society.

Finally, as von Hirsch points out, the benefits and burdens argument, which requires the imposition of some type of punishment, is hard put to justify why it ought to entail such hard treatment as incarceration. "Suppose the offender were formally censured and also required to compensate the victim. Why is this 'disadvantage' not sufficient to satisfy the benefits and burdens theory?"[30] The benefits and burdens position provides no answers to these dilemmas.

Fisse has noted that the arguments against the benefits and burdens position are convincing with regard to individuals, but are not applicable when the offender is a corporation. Unlike crimes committed by individual offenders, offenses committed by corporations result in the "accumulation of an excessively large pool of money, power and prestige for distribution to shareholders, personnel and consumers and other persons who will share in the allocation of corporate resources."[31] When the corporation is not forced to internalize the social costs of the offense through punishment, the individuals who share in the benefits of the crime stand to gain considerably from it. Corporate punishment is justified, then, on the retributive grounds that such advantage as is gained by corporate beneficiaries will result in great inequality in the allocation of social resources.

In spite of the logic of Fisse's claim, it is not clear how this version of corporate retributivism overcomes the criticisms raised by Braithwaite and von Hirsch. Though stated axiomatically, Fisse's proposition that corporate crime leads inevitably to a material accumulation by identifiable individuals is by no means obvious. For example, it is not at all apparent what material advantage was accrued to shareholders and corporate personnel when ARCO released oil into the Chicago Sanitary and Ship Canal.[32] Nor is it clear that a linear path exists between corporate punishment and its impact on corporate beneficiaries so that one could have confidence that any inequality in the allocation of social resources will be removed through corporate cost internalization. Can one have confidence that the burdens of corporate punishment brought on through corporate cost internalization will fall on those beneficiaries who *merit* punishment as the retributive rationale requires? How exactly does corporate punishment remove the material advantages of power and prestige so that "equality" is restored in any meaningful way? Such issues suggest that the problems posed by the benefits and burdens position appear equally complex and troublesome when the offender is a corporation.

MODERN RETRIBUTIVE THEORY: PUNISHMENT AND REPROBATION

Corporate-punishment theorists have been apt to suggest that the difficulties surrounding benefits and burdens arguments provide sufficient reason to dismiss retribution as an unworthy aim of punishment. Yet, retributive theory resists such simplification. One version of retributive theory that is less easy to dismiss shifts attention away from the use of punishment as a means to restore the social balance and toward its use as an appropriate and necessary mechanism for calling attention to the wrongfulness of criminal conduct. This version of retribution, focusing on the condemnatory functions of punishment, is best described by Joel Feinberg and Andrew von Hirsch.[33] Here, the retributive aim of punishment does not serve to justify the hard-treatment component of punishment, but instead serves to justify the censuring element that separates punishment from other public sanctions.

To condemn someone for prior wrong deeds simply for the sake of assigning blame has no meaning by itself. Some value(s) must be promoted by the act of reprobation. If, through condemnation, retributive punishments promote values independent of crime reduction, what might those values be? According to Feinberg, the symbolic public condemnation added to the harsh-treatment aspects of punishment fosters important values in society.[34] First, it allows for authoritative disavowal of the acts of the offender; it announces to others that the government does not condone those actions. Second, the expression of condemnation allows for the vindication of the law. Statutes that are not enforced quickly lose their function, their "character as law." Calling attention to the wrongfulness of conduct through punishment "emphatically reaffirms" the importance of the law. Third, punishment and the expression of moral reprobation allows for the absolution of others, particularly victims, associated with the offense. It calls attention to the moral innocence of others that may be tainted by association with the offensive conduct.

Although not directly tied to crime reduction, the values listed above derived through reprobation do suggest a utilitarianism of a kind, in the sense that they appeal to and promote varying societal interests. When utilitarianism is viewed from this broader perspective, it is difficult to imagine any aim of

63

punishment as being nonutilitarian. One way of considering the distinction between utilitarian rationales and at least this version of retribution is to view it with reference to the victim. Utilitarian rationales, virtually by definition, exclude any explicit consideration of the victim of the offense. The concern is with the amount of punishment necessary to reduce the future likelihood of crime, not with the harm per se inflicted upon the victim, be it the individual, society, or both. Retributive rationales, particularly those that emphasize the "symbolic non-acquiesence" derived through punishment, focus on this harm to the victim, expressing a moral testament to the wrongfulness of the conduct. The public condemnation expressed via punishment thus speaks in the name of the people as the morally appropriate response by authority for the harm inflicted on the victim.[35] Failing to call attention to the moral wrongfulness of the conduct in essence acts to condone the harm and strikes most observers as being a totally inappropriate response.

Punishment entails both condemnation and hard treatment. While both components may exist so as to enhance crime prevention, the condemnatory aspect of punishment has value independent of the preventative element.[36] As von Hirsch notes, the expression of condemnation allows the state to "register disapprobation of such conduct on behalf of its citizens":

> The core conduct with which the criminal law deals is wrongful conduct—conduct that violates the rights of other persons. If the state is to carry out the authoritative response to such conduct—as it must if it visits any kind of sanction upon its perpetrators—then it should do so in a manner that testifies to the recognition that the conduct is wrong. To respond in a morally neutral fashion, to treat the conduct merely as a source of costs to the perpetrator, is objectionable because it fails to provide this recognition. This would, among other things, depreciate the importance of the rights that had been infringed upon by the criminal conduct. Such an objection would be incomprehensible were general prevention the only basis for the criminal sanction.[37]

Desert, Retribution, and Punishment

It is perhaps testimony to the confusion that surrounds the term "retribution" to suggest that the term is better clarified by stating what it is not than by stating what it is. Yet, a good beginning can be made by understanding retributive justifications for punishment as those that are not utilitarian in nature, particularly when utilitarianism is viewed as a response intended to prevent future criminality. Retributive justifications do not find their validity in future crime reduction. Rather, their worth lies in the pursuit of different causes: maintaining principles of justice marked by a balanced social order, as in the Kantian position, or serving to demonstrate public nonacquiescence, symbolized by visiting censure in the name of the public.

To the extent that commentators on corporate punishment have considered the retributive rationale at all, the overriding tendency has been to focus on the dilemmas of the benefits and burdens argument. While the criticisms of this position have been thorough, the result has been to dismiss retributive claims too quickly. In consequence, little attention has been paid to the brand of retributive theory that focuses on the value of reprobation and the condemnatory function of punishment. While the propriety of condemnation for corporate offenses will be explored in greater detail below, suffice it to say at this point that there is nothing which immediately discounts the reprobative value of punishment for corporate offenses. The criminal sanction entails this important element *by definition*, and there is no reason to believe that such retributive justifications as those espoused by Feinberg and von Hirsch are not applicable for all varieties of offenses, corporate or otherwise.

The Role of Desert

Not only have corporate-punishment theorists ignored retributive theories that are reprobative in scope, they have largely failed to consider the role of desert in corporate punishment. Desert is a concept central to most retributive theories, and its importance here is understandable, for desert entails a response directed to an individual by virtue of the quality of that person's act. Retributive notions focus on the wrongfulness of the criminal conduct—on the injustice that is entailed in violating the rules of society. One merits or deserves punishment because his or her conduct was wrong, not because the punishment visited on the offender will promote future law-abiding behavior by the offender or by the public at large. As Feinberg has stated, "utility is not a desert basis for any deserved mode of treatment . . . to say that 'S deserves X because it would be in the public interest' is simply to misuse the word 'deserves.' "[38] Regardless of whether the aim of punishment is to restore the social balance, or to call emphatic attention to the wrongfulness of criminal conduct, both focus on the quality of the act at hand, on the injustice that is its product. That one may be punished at all on such grounds takes meaning only when one considers desert.

To what extent does a retributive justification for punishment influence the primacy of desert concerns in determining the allocation of punishments? Quite obviously, a retributive justification for the general aim of punishment will entail retributive responses to the questions whom do we punish and how much do we punish? Yet, in spite of this point, it is not necessary to claim, as some commentators on punishment for corporate crimes have assumed, that retribution must be sole (or even primary) justification for punishing corporations to justify the distribution of punishments according to desert criteria. We may consider the reduction of unwanted behavior to be a justification as well.[39] At this point, the desire to reduce crime and the propriety of calling attention to the wrongfulness of harmful acts are not incompatible with one another as

aims of punishment. One may claim—without contradic- • • •
tion—that the purpose of imposing hard treatment and censure is to deter crime, and at the same time argue that the
distribution of punishment is to be based only on the seriousness of the offense for which the offender has been found
guilty.

DESERT, RETRIBUTION, AND THE MORAL NEUTRALITY OF CORPORATE OFFENSES

The application of principles of desert in the punishment of
corporations and their agents has also been dismissed on the
grounds that retribution-based punishment places undue emphasis on the moral wrongfulness of criminal conduct. The ob- •
jection is raised that many corporate activities are unwanted,
but lack moral reprehensibility and would thus escape the
criminal sanction if deterrence were excluded as the principal
justification for its application.[40]

Those who reject the application of retributive aims for
corporate-criminal punishment on these grounds generally
take one of two positions. The first is that corporate crime as a • •
general category is not the type of crime that instills a sense of
moral outrage among the public. The second position is that • •
certain unwanted acts (largely economic offenses) committed
by corporations and their agents cover a wide range on a con-
tinuum of moral reprehensibility; certain acts may be unwanted (*mala prohibita*) but not "immoral" (*mala in se*). Thus,
if one accepts these two distinctions as valid, then deterrence,
which focuses on eliminating harmful conduct, might justify
the use of the criminal sanction for such activity, but retribution, with its focus on the justice of condemning morally
wrongful conduct, would not.

The first position—that most corporate offenses as a general
category are "morally neutral"—is exemplified by Yoder's

claim that "there is no clear correlation between what is commercially acceptable vs. legally acceptable behavior," adding that the judiciary shares the view that there is nothing morally reprehensible about corporate crime and that such an attitude works strongly against the imposition of criminal sanctions on retributive grounds.[41]

Yet, there is sufficient evidence in both the literature on corporate crime and on attitudes toward the seriousness of corporate offenses to suggest that such a sweeping generalization is incorrect.[42] The product-defect case involving Richardson-Merrell's production of Mer/29, in which more than five hundred persons developed cataracts from a drug whose previous, but withheld, test reports indicated dangers; the production of the defective Firestone 500 tire, which resulted in at least forty-one deaths; and the financial collapse brought on by the Equity Funding scam all involved significant harm, so as to elicit a general response of reprehensibility.[43] Research on public attitudes toward white-collar crime provides ample evidence to substantiate this point.[44] As Cullen et al. have stated:

> Studies extending back into the 1960s indicate that a substantial percentage of the public favors sending white-collar criminals to jail, particularly when the offense involved holds the possibility of physical injury (e.g., selling contaminated food). . . . Braithwaite . . . reported that "contrary to a widespread misconception, there is considerable evidence to support the view that ordinary people subjectively perceive many types of white-collar crime as more serious than most traditional crime." A comparable analysis by Conklin . . . led to the similar suggestion that there is a "greater degree of public condemnation of business violations than is thought to exist by those who claim that the public is apathetic or tolerant of business crime."[45]

The second position suggests that while activities such as those cited above involve some degree of moral reprehensibility, there is a category of corporate offenses that tend not to elicit strong moral sentiments. Such offenses generally involve economic regulations—antitrust violations, price-fixing, unfair competition, and securities violations. According to Kadish:

> The conduct prohibited by economic regulatory laws is not immediately distinguishable from modes of business behavior that are not only socially acceptable, but also affirmatively desirable in an economy founded upon an ideology (not denied by the regulatory regime itself) of free enterprise and the profit motive. . . . Moreover, in some areas, notably the antitrust laws, it is far from clear that there is consensus even by the authors and enforcers of the regulation—the legislators, the courts and administrators—on precisely what should be prohibited and what permitted, and the reason therefor. And as Freud observed, "If a law declares a practice to be criminal, and cannot apply its policy with consistency, its moral effect is necessarily weakened."[46]

While there may be some agreement that most people do not have strong opinions, moral or otherwise, about such things as export laws, more consensus surely exists with most corporate offenses for which the criminal sanction is now employed. Clearly there is substantial harm generated by the collusion of major corporations to set prices at a level higher than would be expected if the marketplace is operating freely. And, in many respects, that harm goes beyond disruption of the marketplace to something that may be more typically associated with theft or fraud. A similar argument can be made about offenses that disrupt the political system. Bribery and extortion are cases in which the offender gains an unfair advantage over others. The harm may be specific and measurable, as in instances where one rightly deserving of a contract is denied it because another has illegally obtained that award through bribery; or the harm may be more general, in that such conduct violates the sacred trust so vital to our political system. Both political and economic offenses may be viewed as reprehensible, albeit in varying degrees, and subject to condemnation and censure.

Again, the surveys of public opinion concerning the moral and economic costs of certain white-collar crimes bear this out. A canvass of Illinois residents demonstrates that while corporate offenses involving such things as price-fixing and violations of trust elicit less social disapproval than offenses involving physical harm, the public still considers the former morally offensive and supports using criminal sanctions for such misconduct.[47]

The strong empirical evidence flies in the face of the view that the public considers corporate offenses as morally blameless. But the moral-neutrality argument often cited in the literature on corporate punishment is fundamentally flawed in a more important respect. It is frequently claimed that the morally neutral nature of certain corporate offenses entails that deterrence (rather than retribution) *must* be considered the principal aim of the criminal sanction, as if the criminal law implies little or no moral blameworthiness if viewed from this perspective. Yet, this ignores the essential characteristic so clearly emphasized by Henry Hart that "what distinguishes a criminal from a civil sanction is the judgment of condemnation which accompanies and justifies its imposition."[48] No doubt the criminal law is applied for the specific purpose of preventing socially harmful activities from taking place. Yet, labeling such activities as undesirable, to the point of applying the criminal sanction, is also to label those offenses as morally wrong in the general sense of that term.

The argument posed by Kadish notwithstanding, the issue here has nothing to do with whether certain types of offenses can be justified only on the basis of deterrence because of their morally neutral quality. The criminal law is a condemnatory instrument. By definition it implies a morality that labels these

Desert, Retribution, and Punishment

offenses as wrong. This being so, to the extent that certain acts *can* be unwanted yet morally neutral (as certain kinds of regulatory filing requirements might be considered) some other resource, such as the administrative or civil remedy, that does not set a moral tone or carry with it the function of condemnation and censure, must be pursued. The question raised is not which aim justifies the application of the criminal sanction, but whether the criminal sanction can be applied at all. Neither aim of the criminal sanction, deterrence or retribution, would be applicable in such arbitrary cases, for both imply moral wrongdoing.

Two caveats are needed here. First, that the criminal law ••• embodies the notion of moral wrongdoing does not imply that labeling an act a crime represents consensus about the wrongfulness of the behavior. Surely, many behaviors sanctioned as crimes by the state are not immoral to all, perhaps not even to most, but they *are* wrong at least to those who have power to label them as such. It is important not to confuse what the law represents in theory and the means by which the law may be used in practice.

Second, morality is a dynamic concept, at once defining the ••• law and being defined by it. This is nowhere better demonstrated than in the realm of corporate crime, where shifting moral boundaries both invite and limit the application of criminal sanctions.[49] These boundaries do not, of course, shift on their own, but do so within the strong currents of various social forces. Many corporate crimes have been viewed as morally neutral by virtue of the power of corporations to exclude any inference of morality from their actions. Their decisions are "business decisions," operating under constraints of economic laws rather than moral laws. Similarly, opposing social forces (for example, the media and the activities of such key moral entrepreneurs as federal and state prosecutors) act to instill the

71

notion of morality by personalizing the harm and constructing and applying a "vocabulary of deviance" to the facets of the activity that make up culpability.[50] To understand white-collar crime, close scrutiny must be paid to the process by which moral boundaries incorporate given behaviors over time and place. However, this concern does not alter the simple fact that behaviors must first be designated wrong before they can be labeled crimes.

This chapter has examined some of the criticisms of desert as it applies to corporate punishment. It must be emphasized that the role of desert in the sentencing of corporations and their agents becomes applicable when one considers the distribution of punishment—to whom may punishment be applied (only to those who have committed an offense) and to what degree (in proportion to the quality [seriousness] of their offense). Desert holds little meaning by itself when we ask what is the general justifying aim of the institution of punishment; the only possible answer would be because the offenders deserve it. But this raises the further question of why offenders deserve it. Only two responses seem adequate justifications for the institution of punishment, therefore: to prevent crime, and to restore important values, independent of crime control, that are diminished by the commission of crimes.

It is this second aim that is labeled the retributive justification. Yet, as has been demonstrated above, much confusion and debate revolves around the values that are restored through punishment; for example, the public's desire for vengeance (in the most emotional sense of the term), the balance of benefits and burdens that create social order, or the value of symbolic nonacquiescence derived from condemning morally wrongful conduct.

A review of the corporate-punishment literature reveals two significant by-products of this ongoing confusion. First, most writers have focused on either vengeance or Kantian notions of benefits and burdens and have dismissed retribution outright as a justification for corporate criminal sanctions because of the difficult issues posed by such arguments. Second, because the concept of desert has been so closely associated with retribution, the result has been to throw the baby out with the bathwater. Since retribution (or, more specifically, Kantian retribution) fails conceptually as a justification for criminal punishment, the idea of desert, as applied to the question of the amount of punishment, has also been neglected.

This chapter has attempted to clarify some of this misunderstanding. It is suggested here that the dismissal of retribution as an aim of corporate criminal sanctions has been hasty at best. When retribution is viewed as incorporating such functions as symbolic nonacquiescence, it takes on greater meaning. Most significant, there is nothing offensive about this function when applied to corporate misconduct; or, to put it another way, there is nothing unique about corporate crime that would exclude retribution (when viewed from this perspective) as a justification for punishment.

The intent here is not to commend retribution as a justification for corporate punishments that may stand on its own. There are important concerns to be raised about this idea as well, among them the value of reprobation as the only justification, when juxtaposed to the harm that is derived from punishment (at least in the manner it is now imposed). This is precisely the reason that such writers as von Hirsch and Feinberg speak of reprobation as but one function of punishment, to be considered in conjunction with the concern for reducing harmful conduct.

What *is* important to note here is that a retributive justification need not be either only Kantian, or the *only* justification for punishment, to warrant the use of desert criteria in determining the amount of punishment imposed for corporate crime. The reduction of unwanted behavior may be a justification as well. The concept of desert is not grounded *by virtue* of retributive rationale, although most retributive concepts, understandably, speak highly of the importance of desert. Rather, the idea of desert grows out of notions of justice and fairness. Regardless of whether the purpose of punishment is primarily crime prevention or retribution, the fact is that punishment contains a condemnatory function. And as von Hirsch has noted, "it is the condemnatory element that requires punishment to be distributed according to offenders' degree of fault." To base punishment on anything other than the offender's act itself would be to condemn that person *unfairly*.

What impact does this view have on corporate punishment? First, it suggests that both deterrence and desert are justifiable and compatible goals of punishment, albeit at different levels. To the extent that a greater deterrent effect can be achieved, it is by maximizing the imposition of criminal sanctions where applicable, not by maximizing the allocation of punishments for those times in which criminal sanctions are employed. At this level—determining the amount of punishment—principles of commensurate deserts may rightly serve as guides. Given the condemnatory element of punishment, sentences would be allocated according to the seriousness of the offense, and would reflect both ordinal and cardinal proportionality. And finally, to the extent that offenses lack the moral opprobrium warranted by the criminal law, they would require an alternative response, through civil or administrative law, that does not reflect the moral connotations of wrongdoing and stigma that are associated with the criminal law.

CHAPTER 5

Liability and Desert: Are Corporations Worthy of Blame?

THE CONCEPT of just deserts is grounded in notions of individual justice. At its foundation is the belief that the rights of individuals should not be unduly sacrificed for the benefits of the larger society.[1] Utilitarian punishment rationales, on the other hand, subordinate the rights of offenders to the protection of society. The conflict between retributive and utilitarian principles is most clearly evident in addressing the question of on whom punishment may be imposed. While one may hold that punishment serves to reduce unwanted behavior, this crime-control aim is likely to be constrained by retributive principles; punishment should not be imposed on those who are undeserving of the condemnation that is connoted by labeling an individual a criminal and depriving him or her of liberty.

HOLDING CORPORATIONS RESPONSIBLE

The principle that only those who have committed a crime (and who have done so in a certain frame of mind) are liable to punishment is firmly rooted in all civilized justice systems, and I will not explore its merits here.[2] However, much has been written recently about the liability of such nonpersons as corporations. In particular, can the criminal sanction, with its emphasis on moral responsibility, ever be imposed on a corporation, which is incapable of possessing a conscious intent in any normal meaning of that term? Or, to return to the question posed by Edward, First Baron Thurlow, Lord Chancellor of England, "Did you ever expect a corporation to have a conscience, when it has no soul to be damned, and no body to be kicked?" While the question of corporate liability poses no particular dilemmas concerning the feasibility of a desert-based system for individuals involved in corporate crime, the propriety of allocating punishments to the corporations themselves according to blame depends, quite clearly, on whether these corporate offenders can ever be considered blameworthy to begin with.[3]

Although considerable debate still prevails among legal theorists, the law seems clear on this issue.[4] As mentioned earlier, the British and American courts have followed closely with one another on the issue of corporate liability.[5] While first refusing to hold corporations liable for anything other than nonfeasance, the courts, relying heavily on the concept of vicarious liability in the law of torts, soon found it reasonable and proper to hold corporations criminally responsible for certain felonies of which *mens rea* was a necessary element. Attributing *mens rea* to the corporation as the common law has done, however, has been met with skepticism by a number of legal scholars.

Gerhard O. W. Mueller notes that the assimilation of the notion of *mens rea* to the corporation entails that several rather serious conceptual difficulties be overcome.[6] First, the concept of *mens rea* presupposes both the ability to act, which Mueller terms physical movement, and mental self-direction. It would be impossible to attribute *mens rea* to a corporation unless it could first be demonstrated that a corporation can possess the capabilities required to perform an act. But the notion of *mens rea* involves more than action and mental self-direction—it involves a frame of mind, or will. And thus, the second hurdle to overcome concerns the issue of whether a corporation can possess a mind with which it may do such things as will harm, entertain guilt, or have the capacity to obey.[7]

In order to hold someone or something accountable, it must first be demonstrated that the party took the action required to commit the offense. Responsibility cannot be fixed to an actor if there is no evidence that the actor caused or could cause the action to occur. As Mueller has pointed out, the argument that a corporation is, by definition, incapable of acting at all runs contrary to the principles of incorporation.[8] Incorporation takes place, among other reasons, so that the corporation may act in ways that are more effective, more efficient, or otherwise not possible. Actions are done by virtue of incorporation, and they are done in the name of the corporation rather than in the name of particular agents within the corporation. One only need pick up the latest edition of the *Wall Street Journal* to note this point. Such headlines as "PepsiCo May Sell Its Unprofitable Wilson Subsidiary," "United Air Will Retain Some Discounts," or "Phillips Petroleum Files Suit to Block Takeover by Icahn" attest to actions taken by virtue of incorporation and indicate both mental self-direction and physical movement.[9]

Lawrence Haworth has developed the notion of corporate action further.[10] He states that a corporation is said to act, and thus to be held responsible, when the outcome of that activity is perceived in terms of giving credit or blame to the organization and not to its specific members. This credit or blame is said to inhere in the corporation, as opposed to the individuals, when two criteria are satisfied. The first is that the activity represents the outcome of the *pattern* of functions that constitutes the organization's form. The second criterion is that the

quality of the activity depends on the organizational arrangements and patterns and not on the qualities of the specific individuals who are involved in the activity:

> Any pattern of functions is a pattern only if the functions relate with
> each other so as to produce a characteristic result, and this result is
> the function of the pattern considered as a whole but not the func-
> tion of any individual member of the system. It is by deriving this
> characteristic result that we are able to identify the characterizing
> purpose of an organization. The functions of engineer, fireman,
> trainman, switchman, etc., inter-refer so as to make up a *pattern* of
> railroad functions, and they, *as* a pattern, imply the characterizing
> purpose of all organizations which are formed by such a pattern of
> functions. The act of hauling freight is an outcome of that pattern of
> functions; and, in general, any act is an outcome of a certain pattern
> of functions just in case it [the act] fulfills the characterizing pur-
> pose of the organization formed by that pattern of functions.
>   Now we can stop at this point and say that any act which is in the
> indicated sense an outcome of an organization's pattern of func-
> tions is properly attributable to that organization. . . . For the or-
> ganization *is* the personnel and tools as organized or formed, and
> the act results from the fact that the personnel and tools functioned
> in a manner consistent with the organization's form. We know that
> the Pennsylvania Railroad is hauling freight just by knowing that
> this is the name of the organization whose pattern and functions are
> being performed so as to produce that characteristic result. [11]

. . . .   It seems obvious that corporations can and do act. Establishing that they are capable of possessing a conscience where such
things as evil, guilt, and obedience reside has been a much
more difficult task. By and large, the evolution of the common
law demonstrates little considered thought on the matter. As
Mueller notes, "the growth of corporate criminal liability was
fostered by analogies from the law of tort. Many courts simply
failed to appreciate any material difference between the two
bodies of law."[12] To the extent that it was considered, the notion
. . of corporate *mens rea* was thought of primarily as a legal fiction
necessary in order to secure compliance with federal rules and
regulations governing corporations:

Rather than offering a strong philosophical argument of a methodological individualist nature (e.g., that the corporations themselves may be personally responsible), the courts tended to deal on the level of practicality. If any philosophical argument underlies the rules used in these courts, it is probably one that focuses on the efficacy of punishment with particular regard to deterrence. It may be assumed that if corporations are to be held criminally liable, in the broad sense defined by the adoption of rules, for the acts of their employees, corporations will exercise special care, beyond what might be regarded as due diligence, to supervise employee activities.[13]

Yet, the ability of corporate executives to supervise employee activity is suspect.[14] It is not at all certain, for example, that stockholders have the power to control and direct the activities of either those who sit on boards of directors or those who hold executive positions in the corporation. Furthermore, doubts have been raised as to whether high managerial officials have much control, in spite of their diligence, over the actions of their charges in lower-level positions—particularly in corporations that are highly decentralized. Finally, the assumption that criminal liability generates compliance among corporate employees mistakenly assumes that the ultimate impact of the punishment will likely fall on those who are, at least in part, responsible for the acts occurring and will not be passed on to other innocent parties (such as consumers in the form of higher prices).[15]

The Model Penal Code reflects the common law in many ways, but it demonstrates greater concern for establishing corporate liability—a concern that reflects "the guilt-deterrence orientation of the common law of crimes."[16] Section 2.07 of the code states:

(1) A corporation may be convicted of the commission of an offense if:
   (a) the offense is a violation or is defined by a statute other than the Code in which a legislative purpose to impose

liability on corporations plainly appears and the conduct is performed by an agent of his office or employment, except that if the law defining the offense designates the agents for whose conduct the corporation is accountable or the circumstances under which it is accountable, such provisions shall apply; or

(b) the offense consists of an omission to discharge a specific duty of affirmative performance imposed on corporations by law; or

(c) the commission of the offense was authorized, requested, commanded, performed or recklessly tolerated by the board of directors or by a high managerial agent acting in behalf of the corporation within the scope of his office or employment. . . .

(4) (c) "high managerial agent" means an officer of a corporation having duties of such responsibility that his conduct may fairly be assumed to represent the policy of the corporation.

(5) In any prosecution of a corporation . . . for the commission of an offense included within the terms of Subsection (1)(a) other than an offense for which absolute liability has been imposed, it shall be a defense if the defendant proves by a preponderance of evidence that the high managerial agent having supervisory responsibility over the subject matter of the offense employed due diligence to prevent the commission. This paragraph shall not apply if it is plainly inconsistent with the legislative purpose in defining the particular offense.[17]

The Model Penal Code goes beyond vicarious liability to the will of the corporation, albeit in a crude manner, at the level where management decisions are made and can be said to reflect the policy of the corporation itself. The focus here is on the structural positions within the corporation, not on the particular individuals who occupy those positions. Decisions made at this level are granted by the authority vested in the particular office as established in the corporation's management policy. Such decisions represent the mind of the corporation and are assumed to be made in furtherance of the goals and objectives of the corporation itself.[18]

Liability and Desert

Although the concept of corporate personal liability, as established by the Model Penal Code, incorporates values the criminal law attaches to moral blameworthiness to a much greater extent than does the notion of vicarious liability, in many respects it does not go far enough in this regard. As H. L. Leigh has noted, "the question is not whether the relevant human actor occupies a particular place within the corporation, but whether, whatever his title, he exercises substantially autonomous powers in respect to a significant aspect of the corporation's activities."[19] Are there any other methods, then, in addition to the one suggested in the Model Penal Code, that can aid in locating the corporate mind?

Peter French has suggested in *Collective and Corporate Responsibility* that every corporation has an internal decision structure (which he terms the CID structure) that represents "the personal organization for the exercise of the corporation's power with respect to its ventures."[20] Such a structure consists of a flowchart of the corporate decision-making hierarchy that demonstrates organizational responsibility. This flowchart generally defines those levels and positions within the corporation that represent the decision-making processes. The CID structure also involves an additional element—a set of operating rules normally referred to as the corporation's policy. These "internal recognition rules" consist of "procedural recognitors," which demonstrate the collective nature of the decision-making process, and "policy recognitors," which represent the "basic beliefs of the corporation":[21]

> Organizational, i.e., decision flowcharts identify stations and managerial levels and plot the lines of authority, subordination, and dependence among and between such stations within the corporation. . . . The chart clarifies the authority of the actual decision-maker and, of course, identifies the levels and offices to which he must report, to whom or which he is responsible and from whom or

81

which he may expect the credit or the blame, the reward or the punishment after the actions have occurred. These responsibility entanglements as represented on the flowchart partially ensure the corporate character of actions taken, policies and procedures adopted.[22]

With regard to the recognition rules, French elaborates:

> Recognition rules within the Corporate Internal Decision Structure determine and justify the corporate intentional character of corporate actions. They warrant the identification of particular decisions as corporate, but they cannot be justified. That a rule is a recognition rule of CID Structure is a factual matter. We find out what rules of recognition are in place within its CID Structure by consulting the basic operational documents and written policies of a corporation.[23]

··· While the principles stated above help to clarify the ascription of responsibility to the corporation as an entity, it is not yet clear why corporations may be considered appropriate objects of *moral* culpability. To address this question the notion of moral blameworthiness must be examined in more detail. The concept of blame may entail a nonmoral meaning, as in "the hurricane was to blame for the destruction of Padre Island." While the damage to Padre Island may be the product of the storm, the hurricane is not to be held morally blameworthy for the damage. This is so because there is no evidence that it intended (or could even be said to intend) for the destruction to occur. To make responsibility or blame a moral notion requires that the subject in question be capable of directing what it did, or of altering its course, deliberately, so as to cause or prevent the harm from occurring:

> Ascriptions of moral responsibility and blame involve much more than identification of the causes of disapproved events, though they clearly are parasitic upon nonmoral responsibility. A moral responsibility or blaming ascription amounts to the assertion of a conjunctive proposition, the first conjunct of which identifies the subject's

actions with or as the cause of an event and the second conjunct asserts that the action in question was intended by the subject or that the event was related . . . to the intentional act of the subject.[24]

By examining the corporation's internal decision structure it is possible to identify the cause of the offense as being the product of specific corporate (as opposed to individual) actions. Furthermore, and most important, the components of the corporation's internal decision structure—its flow-chart and procedural and recognition rules—are precisely those things that define corporate intention. In the words of French,

> when the corporate act is consistent with an instantiation or an implementation of established corporate policy, then it is proper to describe it as having been done for corporate reasons, as having been caused by a corporate desire coupled with a corporate belief and so, in other words, as corporate intentional.[25]

Whether legal or illegal, the corporation sets certain goals and objectives, and implements a structure and process defined by those components to reach the goals. This makes intuitive sense, since it is on the basis of these components that corporations are judged on a regular basis—by shareholders, regulators, customers, and competitors—as to whether, and to what degree, they accomplished what they intended. Given that corporations are capable of acting with intention and given that corporations are capable of committing harmful acts, it therefore holds that corporations may be held morally accountable for the harms they produce if it can be demonstrated that the harm was, in fact, the product of some form of intent. Determining corporate culpability and its degree for the purposes of sentencing will be addressed in more detail later on. What is important here is the idea that a corporation may be held responsible, both legally (in a nonmoral fashion) and morally when two conditions are satisfied: when the act reflects corporate decisions, and not simply the choices of individuals within the corporation, and when the act is intended by the corporation (either by commission or omission) and is not merely an event attributed to it. Both conditions can be satisfied or not by examining the corporation's internal decision structure.

Is this system of liability an improvement over that proffered by the Model Penal Code? I noted earlier that one of the problems with establishing *mens rea* by identifying the corporate mind with certain high managerial positions, such as a seat on the board of directors, is that corporate policy is often made at levels that are not typically construed as being at the top of the organization. Such is the case when corporations exhibit high decentralization, where locating a management center can be difficult. Yet, by examining the CID structure as described by French, in particular the nonformal decision-making channels, one is better able to identify the roles within a corporation that reflect true corporate policy.[26]

A second problem associated with a doctrine that identifies the will of the corporation according to the structural positions within it is that often, although the position indicates corporate will, the decision itself does not. The corporation is then held accountable for the act, when in fact the act was not representative of corporate policy. Had the act been noticed by those who oversee corporate policy, steps would have been taken to prevent.[27] As French notes:

> What is wanted is a statement that allows the corporation on the basis of established internal policy to rebut the attribution of corporate responsibility of any act of its high managerial staff members working within their defined corporate powers. In short, what is needed is a clear recognition that an act is corporate not only because of its form, but because of the policy it instantiates, displays or manifests.[28]

84

Liability and Desert

By examining the corporate internal decision structure, in particular the policy recognitors, one will be better able to weigh the relevance of the defense that the decision did not reflect corporate procedure. In addition, the establishment of a defense of due diligence will aid in minimizing this problem.[29] A due-diligence defense allows the corporation to rebut the presumption of liability by proving by a preponderance of evidence that it exercised due diligence to prevent the crime. Such a defense requires the corporation to prove that the illegal act had been clearly forbidden, that the corporation had developed and implemented safeguards against corporate crimes, and that those safeguards outlined procedures to evaluate, detect, and remedy any actions indicative of illegal behavior.[30] A due-diligence defense is in keeping with the principles of guilt established in the criminal law. If the corporation can demonstrate that the actions taken were not in keeping with standard policies and established in its ordinary operating procedures, and consequently did not indicate any corporate intent, then the individual actor, and not the corporation itself, should be the party subject to blame.

So far, the concern has been with the issues that surround the establishment of a separate corporate personal liability. The focus has been on the corporation simply because it has, at least in theory, represented what Fisse calls the "blackest hole in the theory of corporate criminal law."[31] As I noted earlier, the concept of corporate liability has grown primarily from utilitarian concerns. At its root is the general belief that individual liability in the corporate context is by itself insufficient to foster either specific or general deterrence. The diffused responsibility, organizational secrecy, resource constraints, and the potential coercion to implement employee reforms have been cited as reasons that corporate liability should work either separately or in conjunction with individual liability.[32] The establishment of a corporate liability has thus been justified so as to expand the deterrent impact of the law.[33] That such a doctrine of liability reflects genuine intent has been secondary to the goals of crime reduction. As we have seen, however, the development of a theory of corporate liability is relevant for retributive reasons as well. Simply put, a corporation may be held worthy of blame as an entity when an examination of its policies, operations, or structure indicates an intent to commit an illegal act. Does this mean that a doctrine of corporate fault based on policies and procedures will be any less effective in reducing corporate crime than a doctrine, such as vicarious responsibility, that is less concerned about establishing genuine corporate intent? This is an empirical question that merits further attention. It may well be that specific intent is not easy to uncover through these procedures and that perhaps all that can be uncovered is evidence of corporate negligence.

Two points may be made here in response. First, as French points out, negligent omissions and commissions will probably still constitute the bulk of corporate liability, and, by and large, such offenses are going to be more socially important than are cases involving higher levels of culpability.[34] Second, the inability to locate intent from the internal operating structure of the corporation does not preclude legal action in the particular case. After all, inability to find a corporate *mens rea* in no way alters the direction that may be taken against individuals acting on the corporation's behalf. Where individuals within the corporation, at any level, demonstrate intent to commit a crime, they too are subject to blame, and they may be held responsible, regardless of whether the corporation itself is accountable.[35] While such an approach may not provide the optimum deterrent effect, the establishment of a realistic corporate *mens rea* is in keeping with the important retributive ideologies that underlie the criminal law.

Finally, although significant steps have been taken to develop sound corporate criminal law, several problems continue to hamper its growth. The issue perhaps of greatest relevance at this point involves the insistence on "strict liability" statutes, whereby liability is imposed for conduct of minimum culpability for certain corporate offenses.[36] There are several arguments for the imposition of strict-liability statutes in the realm of corporate crime. First, it is administratively convenient to hold both corporations and agents acting on their behalf responsible for an offense without allowing the defendant to argue a defense of no intent or mistake. The argument generally runs that the nature of the offense is such that providing defendants with such opportunities would tie up the courts in an unbearable fashion. The second line of reasoning for the imposition of strict-liability standards is based on the need to regulate, rather than to impose blame for, relatively minor activities that pose a potential danger if engaged in without diligence. A third argument incorporates the rules of civil liability as guides for liability in the criminal law. In this instance the courts view liability as placing the risk and the burden of loss on the wrongdoer, rather than allowing that loss to fall on some innocent party.[37] In essence, the loss falls on the party who has the most to gain from the offense. The fourth argument for the imposition of strict-liability standards is that the penal sanctions imposed are sufficiently mild so as to diminish the reprobative force normally associated with criminal punishments. When such mild sanctions exist, the reasoning goes, one may dispense with issues of culpability so as to simplify the process. Finally, and quite opposite the preceding rationale, strict-

87

liability statutes are at times created because the offense in question is deemed so serious that the need to avoid the injury caused by the offense simply outweighs the protections afforded to the accused by requiring proof of intention or lack of care.

The creation of strict-liability statutes in the realm of corporate crime stems in part from a combination of all these reasons. It is clear, however, that such statutes violate principles of justice that are rooted in the retributive philosophy undergirding the criminal law. Unlike treatment under the civil law, criminal punishment is for blameworthy conduct (regardless of the importance of blame). With this in mind it seems inappropriate to punish so as to distribute the loss caused by the offense in some economically distributive fashion. Furthermore, while there are differences in the degree of blameworthiness associated with punishment, it is difficult to argue that there is a point in the application of the criminal law where the loss of liberty, and the stigma associated with criminal conviction and punishment, are deemed minor. The criminal sanction is, by definition, a harsh sanction, and to rely on the criminal law for minor offenses as simply a convenient regulatory tool demeans its importance. Finally, and most important, because the criminal law is reserved for blameworthy conduct, justice requires that blame be imposed only where there is culpability to a high degree. Foregoing high culpability requirements in instances where serious harm is caused or risked contradicts the purposes for imposing a general theory of *mens rea* in the criminal law in the first place. *Mens rea* defenses are entertained when the harm or risk of harm is so serious as to merit the full brunt of the criminal sanction. To forgo *mens rea* requirements for certain offenses because of their seriousness runs counter to this line of reasoning.

Liability and Desert
CONCLUSION

Some corporate legal theorists have raised questions concerning the applicability of principles of commensurate deserts in the allocation of punishments for corporate offenses. The focus of the last two chapters has been on the general *propriety* of the principles of desert in punishing this particular type of criminal activity. By and large, those writing on corporate sanctions have ignored the principles of just deserts in the sentencing of corporations and agents acting on their behalf. This dismissal has been due, in large part, to general misgivings about the role of retribution as a general justification for the institution of corporate punishment and to the problems that surround corporate criminal responsibility.

With regard to this latter concern, the rejection of principles of desert in the allocation of punishments for corporate offenses is largely attributable to the general misgivings about the blameworthiness of "soulless" corporations. By and large, the development of corporate criminal liability has grown out of a general effort to expand the control over ever-increasing corporate power, with the doctrine of vicarious responsibility serving as a fiction to facilitate this end. Given this emphasis on deterrence, the development of a principle of corporate liability that reflects some genuine corporate will or state of mind has not been considered a pressing matter. At least in theory, however, there recently has been an attempt to develop a view of corporate personal liability that comes closer to reflecting true intent. While one may never be completely comfortable with efforts to locate a corporate conscience that is, in any way, similar to the conscience of individual human actors, a theory of corporate liability that focuses on the structure, procedures, and policies of the corporation seems more in line with the general principles of punishment that focus on blame and individual justice than do notions of vicarious liability or those that focus only on the structural positions occupied by the individuals involved.[38]

We have just examined the philosophical issues that confront the development of such a theory—in particular, that corporate offenses can be attributed to a corporation as an entity, and that corporate intentionality (and therefore corporate moral blameworthiness) can be determined by examining the corporation's internal decision structure. There is, however, a general set of concerns with regard to the applicability of desert notions to the punishment of corporations and agents that does not stem from general principles of punishment, but rather involves the practical issues that surround the feasibility of such a sentencing system. Of particular concern are questions regarding the determination of the harm of corporate offenses, identifying the culpability of both the corporation and the individual actor, determining the quantum of punishment, and locating mitigating and aggravating circumstances that are relevant in a desert-based punishment scheme. Let us now turn to these areas.

CHAPTER 6

Assessing the Seriousness
of Corporate Crime:
The Concept of Harm

W HERE utilitarian punishment rationale bases the amount of punishment on forward-crime-control concerns, a desert-based punishment system scales the severity of the punishment to the gravity of the crime. The seriousness of the offense, in turn, is viewed as the combination of two factors: the *harm* or injury wrought or ··· risked by the offense and the degree of *culpability* of the perpetrator.[1] This chapter examines the element of harm, and the means by which harms resulting from corporate crime may be ranked for the purposes of punishment.

Admittedly, the issues involved in ranking corporate crimes differ little from those of ranking common crimes. Ranking generally entails the organized quantitative comparison of items sharing a certain characteristic; it is similar to ordering musical talents, beauty contestants, or street crimes. However, some special considerations plague the assessment of corporate-offense severity: such crimes often result in multi- ·· ple victimization and diffused harm and present problems in locating culpability.

While these features may make the assessment of corporate-offense seriousness more tedious, they are not insurmount-

Just Deserts for Corporate Criminals

able problems. To clarify these specific concerns, I begin by examining the strategies by which offenses may be ranked for the purpose of sentencing.

POPULAR SURVEYS

In the past decade, scholarly attention has been directed at the use of popular surveys as a means of assessing perceived offense severity. Such polls (which use either magnitude estimations, paired comparisons, or categorical scaling techniques) ask population samples to rate the perceived severity of a given variety of crimes, including white-collar offenses. The results of the findings have been applied in a variety of ways: to produce more sensitive measures of changing crime trends, to provide a better understanding of the relationship between consensus and conflict in the criminal law, to provide more information on offense severity and on such things as victimization and the fear of crime, and as a means of allocating scarce criminal-justice resources.[2]

Popular surveys have been suggested as one means by which offenses may be ranked in seriousness for the purposes of punishment.[3] Yet, in spite of the data which suggest that rankings of offense seriousness remain largely stable over subgroups of the population, the usefulness of such surveys for sentencing is limited for several reasons.

First, at least from a desert perspective, offense seriousness is viewed in terms of harm and culpability, where "harm" refers to the injury caused or risked and "culpability" refers to the actor's intent, possibly including motives and circumstances surrounding the commission of the offense. Yet, popular surveys do little to clarify these concepts in the minds of respondents. For the most part, surveys are limited to asking respondents to assign a score representing seriousness, however they define it, to a given type of crime. Consequently, other factors besides harm and culpability can enter into the ranking, lending confusion, if not distortion, to the interpretation of the surveys.

To compound this problem, most surveys define or describe the offenses in a mere one or two sentences. For example, a recent canvass of the perceived seriousness of white-collar offenses described the offenses as

1. Manufacturing and selling drugs known to be harmful to users
2. Causing the death of an employee by neglecting to repair machinery
3. A public official accepting bribes in return for favors
4. An employee embezzling company funds
5. Fixing prices of a consumer product
6. Knowingly selling worthless stocks as valuable investments.[4]

If surveys of offense severity are to be at all helpful in ranking seriousness for desert concerns, a more complete description of the offense must be provided. While such a survey may indeed demonstrate widespread consensus that the knowing sale of contaminated food that results in death is considered more serious than bribing a public official for favors, several crucial factors remain unknown. First, there is no way of telling *why* the respondents rated the offenses the way they did. In such briefly defined offenses, one cannot know whether the respondents ranked the offenses according to the perceived physical harm produced by the acts, what interests they considered in the assessment of harm, and how, or whether, they took into consideration issues of culpability, including such factors as motive, circumstances, or excuses.[5]

Even if culpability factors were considered, there is no way of knowing how such factors were ranked, or whether they

Just Deserts for Corporate Criminals

were considered in any manner similar to what is acceptable within the generally broad interpretations afforded them in the criminal law. It is quite apparent that judges themselves have widely differing views as to the definitions of *scienter* requirements in the criminal law. To the extent that single-sentence descriptions include such words as "willfully," "knowingly," and "negligently," it is doubtful that lay persons are going to have a clear understanding of the importance of such terms or the distinctions between them.

Another factor that affects the ranking of various offenses, particularly with regard to corporate crime, is the image of the offender. Lending money at illegal rates presents to many a picture of the "Godfather," and all the stereotypes of "mob guys" come to mind. Drug addicts conjure up images of glazed-eyed figures who break into homes or commit acts of violence as a result of their addiction. The price-fixing violator is the guy next door (assuming one lives in a middle- to upper-class neighborhood) with whom a strong affiliation exists, or the present-day robber baron, immune from the law, who steals from the law-abiding to satisfy his own greed. The seriousness of the offense, then, takes on different meaning and incorporates prejudices or philosophies not directly related to the act itself.

Perhaps more important, perceptions of offense seriousness are limited to being what they are—perceptions.[6] They do not necessarily represent the actual seriousness of the offense in terms of the harm that was caused or risked, or the culpability of the actor. Yet, it is *actual* harm and culpability on which punishment should be based. Greater attention must be paid to the determination of the actual harm that occurs with different types of offenses, and more information is needed on the ways in which such a determination may be used in ranking offense seriousness for the purpose of punishment.

94

Assessing Corporate Crime

What seems apparent is that current surveys on offense seriousness supply neither adequate nor accurate information on seriousness as it is defined from a desert perspective. Yet, even if they did, such information in and of itself would still be of little use. Even excluding the problems of culpability, understanding harm and ranking it requires that principled consideration be given to the priority of interests affected:

> Empirical inquiry into criminal harm must be supplemented by value judgments. . . . Different crimes injure different interests. Car theft involves a substantial loss of property; armed robbery usually entails much less money lost, but a threat to the person's life. Most of us would rate car theft as much less serious than robbery, because we consider the interest in personal safety to be more important than that in common items of property. But more thought is needed as to *why* we assign these priorities.[7]

While this area remains largely virgin territory, a number of scholars have begun to pay greater attention to it. Drawing on the writings of Joel Feinberg and Andrew von Hirsch, attention is now directed to the concept of criminal harm, the issues pertaining to the ranking of interests, and the application of these issues to corporate crimes.

CRIMINAL HARM AND THE RANKING OF INTERESTS

The concept of harm is a complex and varied one. Like concepts of good and bad, right and wrong, benevolence and greed, harm involves considered judgment. The job of scaling harms not only entails the understanding of the *extent* of the injury caused or risked, but also involves an understanding, and ultimately, a ranking of the different *interests* injured. Yet, in spite of its importance to criminal law, the concept of harm has not received the scholarly attention it deserves. As Gerhard O. W. Mueller has noted, "the principle of harm is the most underdeveloped concept in our criminal law."[8] While British as well as German legal theorists have for some time struggled with the notion of harm, American theories of harm are relatively recent. In perhaps the first major treatise on harm by an American legal scholar, Jerome Hall advanced the notion that harm entails both the "fact," or the material injury, caused by the offense and normative judgments involving incorporeal interests and values.[9] According to Hall, "harm must be stated in terms of intangibles such as harm to institutions, public safety, the autonomy of women, reputation and so on. In short, harm entails the loss of value."[10] Furthermore, the value or loss of value depends on how people perceive them, making harm a "complex of fact, value and interpersonal relation."[11]

Mueller advanced the notion of harm as espoused by Hall, positing that harm entails three levels of abstraction.[12] First, harm arises as a simple breach of the law. According to this view, rejection of the rules of the state is itself harmful, independent of any other feature of the harm. On a second level, harm involves the destruction of legally protected interests in the social context. Thus, when a person is murdered or physically injured, all of society is harmed by virtue of the value loss to general interests in life and physical welfare. Finally, harm may occur to the specific individual protected by the provision incorporated in the criminal law.

That the harm caused by a criminal act entails more than just a broken bone, blackened skies, the loss of $500, or the theft of a Cutlass station wagon is certainly important with regard to the manner in which those injuries are assessed and ultimately scaled. Each of the acts that produced these harms represents an infringement on some value or combination of values considered vital to the maintenance of social existence. Yet, what exactly are those values, and how may they be scaled? This question must be addressed before one may engage in the task of scaling corporate offense seriousness for the purposes of punishment. This chapter will examine the works of those who have considered the meaning of harm, and from that work attempt to suggest some meaningful guidelines by which harms, and in particular corporate harms, can be assessed for the purposes of punishment.

John Kleinig states that the notion of harm is best understood in the context of infringement on certain generic or universal interests, which he terms welfare interests:

> Welfare interests, in their foundational aspect, are those interests which are indispensable to the pursuit and fulfillment of characteristically human interests, whatever those interests might be. Being foundational, their satisfaction is not to be identified with a person's happiness or well-being so much as the conditions which make happiness and well-being possible.[13]

Kleinig does not specify exactly what those generic interests are, or should be, but he does suggest that they might include such things as bodily and mental health, normal intellectual development, adequate material security, stable and nonsuperficial interpersonal relationships, and a fair degree of liberty.[14]

Joel Feinberg maintains a similar perspective with regard to the existence of particular generic interests and their importance as key requirements for the sustenance of well-being.[15] He lists such concerns as the interest in one's physical health and vigor, the integrity and normal functioning of one's body, the absence of absorbing pain and suffering or grotesque disfigurement, minimal intellectual acuity, emotional stability, economic sufficiency, a tolerable social and physical environment, and minimal freedom from interference and coercion.[16]

Ranking Interests

Given that the criminal sanction is directed toward protecting specific generic interests, the question remains, What is the relative order of importance of these interests themselves?[17] How might these interests be ranked so as to provide a starting point for the assessment and scaling of certain kinds of corporate offenses?

Andrew von Hirsch has pointed out the difficulty of ordering these basic vital interests. He cites as an example the problems encountered in grading such generic interests as physical integrity and property. While in most cases harm to physical integrity would be considered more serious than harm to property, such would not always be the case; substantial harm to property might outweigh relatively minor harms to physical integrity. Second, he notes that in a free society, particularly one characterized as having a pluralistic culture, individuals *should* have the right to choose which interests are most important in their lives. Thus, according to von Hirsch, "we want a theory of harm . . . that makes allowance for differences in how people value the worth of life's goods."[18]

Levels of Harm to Interests: Welfare, Security, and Accumulative Interests

Feinberg has developed a tripartite grading model that serves to explain how different interests may be compared for the purposes of assessing harm.[19] Although Feinberg's model specifically addresses which types of harmful conduct should be legislated against, von Hirsch has incorporated the model in the scaling of offense seriousness for the purpose of sentencing.[20]

The concept of *welfare* interests serves as the starting point for Feinberg's model; such concerns "provide the generalized means to the advancement of a person's more ulterior interests."[21] A welfare interest is the basic or acceptable minimum of any given interest necessary in order to live life productively. For example, the welfare interest in physical well-being consists of the minimal conditions of physical health necessary in order to pursue one's basic aims or goals in life. Harms to welfare interests represent the most damaging types of injury and would therefore be considered the most serious in terms of the criminal law. Offenses to this level of interest, with the requisite culpability, would receive that most severe punishment.

Feinberg terms the second level of interests *security* interests. While the welfare interest in physical well-being concerns the minimum level of well-being that is tolerable, the security interest represents additional protection with respect to that interest and affords individuals a great margin of comfort from that minimum line.[22] To use Feinberg's term, the security interest "cushions the welfare interest" and allows an individual to live his or her life more securely. For example, certain types of physical assaults or health and safety violations that, when committed with the required degree of culpability, inflict non-life-threatening bodily injury would represent harms to this level of interest. Von Hirsch terms these offenses "intermediate harms," and they would merit the next level of punishment severity.

"Beyond the basic interests (represented by welfare and security interests) people seek to accumulate the various good things in life."[23] These pleasures, best characterized as nonessential, represent *accumulative* interests. A theft of one's credit cards, for instance, constitutes a harm to this third level. While these concerns merit protection, they are not as crucial to the quality of one's existence as are welfare interests or security interests. As a consequence, such harms merit the least severe punishment, given the requisite culpability. Feinberg discusses the differences between these levels of interest:

> Everyone has a derivative interest . . . in possessing more money or liberty than he actually needs, as a "cushion" against possible

future invasion of his welfare interest in having enough to get along. Consequently, the closer are one's assets (in money, liberty, or health) to the minimal line, the more harmful are depletions of them above the minimal line. For all welfare interests there is some analogue of the principle of the diminishing marginal utility of money. The legislative interest-balancer then will ascribe some weight to all legitimate interests including all interests in liberty, but he will ascribe greater weight to the welfare interest in liberty than to the security interest in cushioning that welfare interest, and greater weight to the interest in securing minimal liberty than to the interest in accumulating extensive transminimal liberty or "as much liberty as possible."[24]

Feinberg's categories provide a useful first step in the ranking of certain kinds of harms.[25] Yet, a lingering problem remains. To this point, no distinction has been made regarding the relative importance of generic interests within these categories. Are harms to the welfare interest in personal property equal in seriousness to harms to the welfare interest in physical integrity or well-being? Are harms to the security interest in liberty equal in seriousness to harms to the security interest in property? As much as one would encourage a theory of harm that allows for individual differences, some further grading of generic interests seems required, and is, in fact, implicit in the criminal law. As von Hirsch acknowledges, the criminal law has treated violent offenses as more serious than even the worst of property crimes.[26] While it may be possible to speculate on the reasons for this ranking, no systematic rationale has been devised. A next step in developing a theoretical foundation for the ranking of harms, therefore, would be to examine in a more considered way the means by which these fundamental interests can be graded.

Let us begin here by examining interests in terms of their *inclusiveness*. The thwarting of certain generic interests will entail impairment to other generic interests as well. The clearest example is the harm to life. Obviously, when one's life has been taken away, all other interests are affected. Thus, the more interests included in the welfare interest, the more harmful the interference with that welfare interest would be. Suppose we choose for the purpose of illustration several of the generic interests suggested by Feinberg that merit protection by the criminal law:

Generic Interests
in physical health and vigor
in the absence of obsessive pain
in the absence of grotesque disfigurement
in intellectual competency
in economic sufficiency
in a tolerable environment
in minimal political liberty

Suppose one considers the relative importance of the interest in intellectual competence. In this case, harm to intellectual competence would not seem to lead to harms in the interests concerning physical health and vigor, obsessive pain, or gross disfigurement. But it may likely lead to harm to economic sufficiency. The harm caused would not, of course, be as extensive as in the case of the taking of a life, but one could reasonably expect that a harm to intellectual competence would typically affect the likelihood of one's obtaining the minimum level of economic sufficiency available to others not so harmed. Similarly, harm to intellectual competence is likely to damage one's emotional stability as well. Emotional stability is, of course, a complex notion entailing many different factors. But a reasonable argument could be made that one of the conditions that makes for emotional stability is the realization that our generic interests are available and protected in some formal way. In a similar fashion, harm to economic sufficiency is likely to entail harms to other interests, including emotional stability, physical health and vigor, and intellectual competence.

This discussion suggests guides, based on the notion of inclusiveness, by which interests may initially be ranked. A model similar to this may also be used to represent the relationship between these vital interests and the ulterior interests they are said to represent. These generic concerns serve as the minimum necessary conditions for the pursuit of more focal or ulterior interests. Yet, generic interests are not equal in the degree to which they allow for the development and expression of ulterior interests. Obviously, one cannot pursue any goal, aspiration, or dream if his or her life has been taken away. Nor can one expect to fulfill the hopes of playing the piano, having a family, sailing a boat, or traveling to Europe if one has suffered such extensive bodily harm as to be confined permanently to a bed or wheelchair. Compare these harms, for instance, with the harm to the vital interest in the possession of personal property. While interference with that interest is indeed harmful, it is not likely that it affects the range of activities and interests that are protected by the fundamental interest in physical well-being. Feinberg notes that one of the ways in which opposing interests that are invaded to the same degree may be evaluated for their relative importance is by examining their "vitality."[27] This notion of vitality is similar to the notion of inclusiveness. Interests differ in their vitality to the extent that harm to them produces greater or lesser consequences throughout the entire "network" of interests.

Inclusiveness, it appears, is itself determined by two factors: the extent or *comprehensiveness* of the consequences felt throughout the network, and longevity or *permanence* of those consequences. Thus, harm to physical well-being greatly affects a vast spectrum of personal interests and also typically leaves lasting effects; one might never recover from the harm inflicted. On the other hand, harm to privacy or property appears, at least on its face, to inflict a lesser degree of harm to other interests within the network, and typically suggests that things may once again be restored to normal, or close to normal.

So far we have focused on some possible guides by which interests may be prioritized and ranked. Using Feinberg's threefold model, interests can be ranked depending on whether they constitute welfare interests, security interests, or accumulative interests. I have also suggested that the interests may be further ordered according to their inclusivity, where inclusivity is determined by the comprehensiveness and the permanence of the consequences. These concepts then serve as the guides by which the interests harmed by various offenses can be ranked in relative order of importance. Offenses can then be analyzed with reference to the harm that is typically produced or risked by their occurrence and can be located on the scale of harm accordingly. Yet, before efforts are taken to apply these concepts in the ranking of corporate offenses, it is important to note and attempt to address some special features of corporate crimes that must be considered in the assessment of seriousness. These have to do with multiple victimization, diffuse victimization, collective harms, and assessing the harm of administrative violations.

ASSESSING CORPORATE-OFFENSE SERIOUSNESS; SPECIAL CONSIDERATIONS

Multiple Victimization

A distinguishing feature of many types of corporate crimes is that a single offense often injures multiple victims. The tendency here is to think of worst-case scenarios, such as the gas leak in Bhopal, India, that immediately killed approximately two thousand people and seriously injured thousands more. Yet even crimes that do not cause such extensive injury still involve, in typical instances, more than one victim. How would the guides outlined here respond to the problem of multiple victimization?

It has been suggested that the offense-seriousness scale begin with the ranking of the relative priority of interests affected and the degree to which the harm to an interest affects the welfare, security, or accumulative levels of that interest. When an offense injures multiple victims, the first step in the ranking entails locating the seriousness of the harm relative to the interests injured, leaving out, for the moment, the number of people who have been harmed in such a manner, since the number of victims does not concern the gravity of the harm per se but, rather, the extent of it.

The multiple-victimization component can then be incorporated into the scale as an aggravating factor to be added to the original level of harm. If two offenses are ranked similarly with respect to the harm typically caused or risked, but only one involves multiple victims, the act involving multiple victims would receive a higher serious ranking and consequently merit more severe punishment.

Diffuse Victimization and Collective Interests

The theory outlined so far is limited to offenses that victimize individuals, involving specific kinds of harms (mainly those to physical well-being, safety, and personal economic stability). Yet, it was noted earlier that a feature of some types of corporate crime is that the harm caused by the offense may be relatively slight to a single victim, but may be serious when the collective interest is considered. Collective interests are those that transcend an individual to become concerns and interests shared by the population at large. An example of such an offense is price-fixing. Here the harm to a single consumer may be small—a unit increase of three cents, for example—yet the overall harm caused by the increase may result in a profit of millions of dollars. Recalling the words of C. Wright Mills (written perhaps with apologies to Woody Guthrie's "Ballad of Pretty Boy Floyd"), is it "better to take one dime from each of ten million people at the point of a corporation than $100,000 from each of ten banks at the point of a gun?"[28] How may a seriousness scale account for the former harm?

Quite obviously, price-fixing or other offenses that render aggregate harm are best characterized by the sum total of the damage done by the particular offense. To do otherwise would fail to capture the essence of the offense. Two corporations that agree to fix retail prices do so with the understanding that the purpose of the conspiracy is to reap large amounts of money, not to fraudulently overcharge an individual customer a nickel. Overcharging one customer serves as the mechanism by which the companies can achieve their goal, but it is not the goal itself.

Yet, harm entails an understanding of both the injury inflicted and the interest affected. The interests affected by corporate crimes with diffused victimization vary greatly, and how one ultimately interprets the interests harmed by diffused-victimization offenses will produce significantly different punishment responses. A single case of price-fixing at one level (a unit increase of three cents) produces harm, but harm only to a collective interest. When that offense is viewed in terms of the aggregate harm (as a $100,000 theft), the interest shifts as well. The harm in such an instance is no longer characterized with respect to a specific individual, but is best depicted as one variant of collective harm. At this point, however, the scale is limited to offenses that victimize individuals, and does not incorporate harms to a group. What is needed, therefore, is a coherent theory of collective interests that may then be incorporated into a similar scale. Clearly, many of the harms to individual interests are likewise harms to collective interests, since the public at large has a stake in the obeisance, or lack thereof, of the laws protecting individual-welfare interests. But the notion of collective interests (or, better yet, *collective harms*) goes beyond this to include harms that are not directed to any specific individual, but rather, in the words of Jeremy Bentham, are directed "to an unassignable indefinite multitude of the whole number of individuals of which the community is composed, although no particular individual should appear more likely to be a sufferer by them than another."[29] Such harms to collective interests involve such offenses as pollution, tax evasion, and political corruption, where specific collective values are infringed upon, as well as "aggregate" harms, which involve a multitude of trivial harms (such as those caused by price-fixing).[30] As a beginning point in assessing the relative priority of collective interests, guidelines similar to those suggested for individual interests may be developed. More problematic, however, is the question of how collective interests compare to individual interests. Addressing this issue would require consideration of the reasons that interests are considered collective to begin with. While these concerns are beyond the scope of this study, they merit further discussion and research.

Administrative Violations

Corporate offenses involving safety, maintenance, and reporting violations are procedural or administrative in nature and present no specific harm in and of themselves, but serve as a means of reducing the risk of the danger of the activity with which they are associated. These offenses merit close scrutiny from a desert perspective, where the condemnatory expression of the criminal sanction is emphasized. Yet, clearly, many of these offenses involve grave risk of loss (both financially and physically) and do merit punishment regardless of the justification one has for the aim of punishment. How are such procedural or administrative offenses to be ordered in terms of seriousness?

A first step in this rating involves a ranking of the resultant harms on the basis of the interests affected by the violation. Thus, a reporting violation concerning safety procedures to be followed in the operation of a nuclear-power plant is more serious than a reporting violation concerning financial statements filed with the Securities and Exchange Commission, since physical safety represents a more important interest in general than economic stability. Thus, the greater the *gravity* of the harm (where gravity is measured by the interests affected), the greater the need for procedural guidelines regulating that activity and, consequently, the greater the seriousness in failing to follow those guidelines.

More is needed than this, however. Certain actions are more likely to produce undesired consequences than are other actions, regardless of the results. Therefore, the *probability* of an injury taking place must also be considered in the assessment of seriousness; the greater the chance of a harm resulting from an offense, the more serious the violation must be considered.

Finally, both the gravity and the probability of the harm must be weighed together. These two factors compounded represent the *risk* of the harm. Thus, the greater the risk of the harm, the greater the seriousness of the violation and the more punishment it would merit.[31]

These principles may serve as useful rules to follow in determining the harm for offenses that are administrative in nature.

However, there are still difficulties left unresolved. One perplexing problem involves the means by which probability is calculated. Differing bases for risk will lead to different probabilities. Take as an example the production of a defective automobile. If the concern is only with the probability of one person dying as the result of the manufacture of the car, it can be safely concluded that the probability of risk is 100 percent—a very high probability indeed. If, however, the probability of loss of life is considered in terms of a given number of automobiles manufactured (say, one person dying for every ten thousand defective cars made), then the likelihood is that the rate will be much lower. In fact, the probability may be negligible.

The question concerning the determination of probabilities raises the more dynamic issue of the process of interest balancing in general. One of the troubling features of many types of corporate activity is that the conduct itself creates some danger (where the exact nature of the harm may or may not be known), yet also carries with it certain social utility. How is it possible to account for the social utility of the conduct in calculating the magnitude and risk of harm—particularly where the interest served by the conduct is different from the interest harmed by the conduct? The production of automobiles provides not only jobs, but also the means of transportation for a large number of people. If there is some question about the safety of a particular car, some calculation is inevitably made regarding the likelihood of someone being harmed by the defect, weighed against the benefits of the car to the public, the cost of recalls and retooling, and the benefits derived by the population from driving that car.[32]

AN OUTLINE OF GUIDES

The assessment of harm for the purposes of establishing a desert-based punishment system requires not only that the myriad harms are outlined clearly, but also that the different interests affected by the harms are scaled in some principled fashion. On the basis of the writings of such theorists as Feinberg, Kleinig, and von Hirsch, some general maxims to begin gauging and balancing the seriousness of different types of harms resulting from corporate offenses may be summarized: • • • • •

1. Harm is best understood in the context of impairment or damage to specific interests of individuals or of collectives.

2. The concept of harm is useful only in terms of "general rules" that incorporate notions of "standard persons." This generalization is in keeping with the criminal law, which uses the concept of standard persons in a wide variety of areas.

3. Harms may be scaled by whether they constitute damage to one's welfare, security, or accumulative interests, where a welfare interest represents the minimal tolerable level of a given interest needed in order to live decently, a security interest represents a degree of safety (or cushion) from the welfare level, and the accumulative interest represents those pursuits that make life enjoyable but that are not vital to the maintenance of a minimum livelihood or to the cushion which protects that livelihood. Holding culpability constant, harms to each of these three levels of interest rank in seriousness in descending order.

4. Interests within each level—welfare, security, and accumulative—vary in priority and thus merit ranking in some relative order of importance. Their significance can be gauged by examining the following criteria:

    a. *The "inclusiveness" of the interest*—the degree to which harm to one welfare interest results in damage to other welfare interests.

    b. The notion of inclusiveness may also be used with regard to the relationship between welfare interests and the ulterior interests they are said to represent. The greater the impact on other goals and aspirations making up the "interest network" the greater the harm is.

c. The concept of inclusiveness includes, or is in part determined by, the *comprehensiveness* of the harm, as well as the *permanence* of the harm. Comprehensiveness entails the extent of the consequences to other interests. Permanence entails the longevity of the harm to the other interests affected.

5. Some harms, often harms caused by corporate misconduct, have no immediate identifiable victims. The harm, instead, is to collective interests. Such harms include such offenses as bribery, tax evasion, or certain types of air pollution. The consideration of collective interests in the assessment of seriousness raises two concerns:

a. As with individual welfare interests, there is a plurality of community interests that must be ranked in order of importance. Community interests may be scaled in relative order of importance in the same fashion as individual interests, where the harm is examined through its impact on the network of community interests. Particular attention would thus be paid to the comprehensiveness of the harm and its permanence.

b. Also to be considered is the relative importance of community interests, compared to individual interests. Such a consideration requires, in theory, that attention be given to the functions and purpose of the collectivity. However, it may also be possible to rate the collective interests with respect to their role in the attainment or freedom of pursuit of individual interests.

6. Finally, corporate offenses often take place in the context of the provision of socially useful services and products. This is particularly true with regulatory offenses, where an in-

dustry or a corporation is required to follow certain guidelines in order to minimize the potential harm that may result from misconduct. One means by which regulatory offenses can be scaled involves a close examination of the corporate activity at hand:

a. The greater the *gravity* of a possible harm the greater the need for procedural guidelines regulating the activity, and thus the greater the harm in failing to follow those guidelines.

b. The greater the *probability* of a harm occurring, the more serious the regulatory offense may be considered.

c. Most important, the greater the *risk* of a harm, where risk is determined by gravity and probability taken together, the more serious is the violation of procedural guidelines.

These principles serve as a possible starting point for the assessment and scaling of harms. How might a sentencing body use these principles, and what problems is the group likely to encounter?

A model that incorporates these ideas would begin with an initial effort to list and rank the interests that merit protection through the criminal sanction. Such an endeavor, undertaken by an actual sentencing commission, would, of course, entail disagreement. Underlying this ranking process, however, is the assumption that a commission can come up with some form of consensus.

Although there is likely to be a variety of generic interests that may be considered, suppose, hypothetically, the commission came up with five important interests and, using the concepts of comprehensiveness and permanence, ranked them in descending order of importance:

1. Physical well-being
2. Economic security
3. Emotional stability
4. Tolerable environment
5. Privacy

Having ranked the concerns themselves, the next step is to rank them according to Feinberg's tripartite model. Levels of harm are thus expressions of infringements to welfare interests, security interests, and accumulative interests. The scale would begin with the ranking of welfare, security, and accumulative interests so that the most serious offenses would be those that harmed the welfare interests of the five generic concerns outlined above; the intermediate level of seriousness would contain those offenses that violate the security interests of those generic concerns, and so on.

Having established the components of the scale that are to serve as guides to assess and rank the seriousness of offenses, the next step would be to analyze the various types of offenses on the basis of the interests affected and the level of harm that typically takes place, so as to fit them on the scale.

Three problems crop up and are worthy of reiteration. First, given the complexity of many corporate crimes, defining the gradients of harm (in other words, which offenses violate welfare interests, security interests, and accumulative interests) will be complicated. Not only is there certain to be considerable disagreement as to the differences between these levels, but, more significant, the range of the behavior in each is generally so large as to incorporate all these levels either simultaneously or at different times. It would not be accurate, for example, to claim that a typical violation of the Clean Air and Water Act damages welfare interests in physical well-being, and should therefore be located accordingly on the scale. Perhaps much more so than with common offenses, the concept of an "average" harm from these crimes is unclear. Under the provisions of the Clean Air and Water Act, such offenses may be visibly irritating, they may cause minor physical ailments, and they may even lead to death.

Second, it seems apparent that in attempting to assess the level of interest harmed by the offense much depends on who the victim is. This question is most evident in the assessment of harm caused by economic violations. Does an offense, say, stock fraud resulting in a loss of $10 million, differ in seriousness if the victims in one instance are institutional clients, such as brokerage houses, or, in another case, individual investors whose life savings were lost? From a perspective of welfare, security, and accumulative interests, it certainly does. The $10 million loss to institutional investors is in all likelihood damage to a security interest, if not an accumulative interest. A $10 million loss representing the life savings of individuals is undoubtedly harm to a welfare interest in economic stability. Much more consideration must be paid to the differences with regard to the victim.

Similarly, the third issue concerns the collective harm caused by many of these crimes. A number of these offenses, such as economic crimes (for example, restraint of trade), affect individuals, but are perhaps best described with reference to the harm they cause to collective interests (for example, the free-enterprise system). No simple answers emerge as to how these collective interests are to be incorporated into the scale of offense seriousness.

With these issues in mind, several points are clear from this brief analysis concerning the general assessment of corporate-offense seriousness. First, much more needs to be learned about the extent of harm done in corporate offenses. It is a relatively simple task to rank interests, albeit that ranking will entail disagreement.[33] It is more problematic to begin to correlate the harm caused by the specific offenses with the interests meriting protection by the criminal sanction. This is especially true when one attempts to make distinctions between types of victims and attempts to get a better understanding of the distinctions between harms to welfare, security, and accumulative interests with respect to this activity. More research needs to be conducted in this area, exploring such questions as the impact and consequences of such acts as pollution, fraud, and corruption. Simply put, making distinctions between harms to welfare interests, security interests, and accumulative interests is a process of refining the concepts of harm. Making refinements, however, implies that there is a basic understanding of the types and consequences of these activities.

This caution does not suggest that there is no knowledge of the ramifications of these acts or that the distinctions are meaningless. Because there is no cure for cancer does not mean that no efforts should be made to try to stop the disease; one proceeds on the basis of what is known at the time. As more knowledge is gathered, refinements can be made. Nor do the issues raised above suggest that a sentencing body cannot begin to make considered choices on the ranking of interests in a coherent fashion. Exact calculations by which all interests can be scaled in precise degrees seems impossible. Yet, the inability to derive specific formulas does not lessen the significance of what has been attempted here. What is important is the notion that any effort to scale harm involves some degree of judgment, and, therefore, some degree of arbitrariness is certain to occur. Yet, some procedures are more arbitrary than others. A process that involves some degree of systematizing—incorporating considered principles and established parameters—is less arbitrary than a process without rules and guidelines. Feinberg has summarized the problem eloquently:

Assessing Corporate Crime

It is impossible to prepare a detailed manual with the exact "weights" of all human interests, the degree to which they are advanced or thwarted by all possible actions and activities duly discounted by objective improbabilities mathematically designated. Drafting legislation can never be made as rote as cooking a casserole by the provision of some analogue of a cookbook of recipes. In the end, it is the legislator himself, using his own fallible judgment rather than spurious formulas and "measurements," who must compare conflicting interests and judge which are the more important. We can only discuss in a general way how legislators can and do go about it, which "dimensions" of interests are relevant, and what "interest-balancing" must involve.[34]

CHAPTER 7

Culpability and Corporate-Offense Seriousness

OFFENSE seriousness is defined by the harm of the crime and by the culpability of the actor. The degree of blame or fault merited by any given conduct depends on the intention of the agent, the agent's motive for the conduct, and the circumstances surrounding the act. Yet, while these components of criminal fault are of vital importance in the substantive law, their specific application to sentencing has not kept pace.[1] This chapter explores the application of notions of criminal fault in the assessment of corporate-offense seriousness.

A crucial notion in the substantive criminal law (as it relates to most common offenses) is that criminal liability to punishment is affected by the intentions of the actor who commits the crime. With some exceptions, what the actor meant to accomplish by his or her act determines whether he or she can be held liable to punishment for it. The intention of the actor is not limited to the threshold question of liability, however. It is also relevant to the issue of how much one should be punished. One is considered to be less blameworthy, and therefore subject to less severe punishment, if the offense was committed recklessly, as opposed to purposefully.

Yet, as much as these distinctions are evident in the substantive corporate criminal law, it is not sufficient merely to interpret statutory provisions regarding intent and apply them to the sentencing process. The very nature and purpose of the intent requirements in the law make such an application undesirable for several reasons.

First, legislative provisions concerning corporate conduct include a mixed bag of intent criteria, particularly as the provisions concern the conduct of direct actors. As with statutes involving common crimes, corporate criminal statutes have adopted any number of standards, including willfulness, knowledge, recklessness, negligence, carelessness, or strict liability. As testimony to the problem, the National Commission on Reform of Federal Criminal Laws found seventy-eight different combinations of words delineating degrees of fault in the various federal statutes.[2] Consequently, different courts will interpret these standards differently.[3]

To complicate matters further, many of the statutory definitions of corporate crimes combine degrees of fault or have not bothered to specify any intent requirement, leaving the courts to infer their own requirements.[4]

Finally, statutes vary in the degree to which they distinguish between corporations as entities, between direct actors within the corporation, or between direct actors who authorize the illegal activity and indirect actors who carry out the policy.

Given these problems, existing definitions of offenses provide little guidance for a sentencing commission—particularly one that is concerned with principles of desert. A first step in the delineation of culpability for the purposes of sentencing would be to redefine offenses related to corporate crime in a manner that brings some understanding and consensus to the differences in the degrees of fault.[5] Attempts at such redefinitions have been made. The Model Penal Code, for example, has delineated four culpability levels—purpose, knowing, recklessness, and negligence—that are applicable to each of the *actus reus* components (conduct, circumstances, and result).[6]

While many of the statutory definitions have lumped these distinctions together, it is still feasible for a sentencing commission to adopt these standards and apply them individually in assessing offense seriousness for the purposes of sentencing.[7] Yet, how are these distinctions to be made? What components of the corporation's behavior or of the behavior of the individuals within the corporation are to be considered in determining these different degrees of fault? Since these factors differ (depending on whether the actor is a corporation or an individual within the corporation), each must be examined separately.

CORPORATE CULPABILITY

Distinguishing degrees of fault for the purposes of sentencing makes little sense if the principles underlying the idea are not relevant to the general system of corporate liability. Why scale punishments according to levels of intent if intent is of little concern at the threshold question of liability to punishment to begin with? Before one can seek any kind of distinctions between degrees of fault, it is necessary to examine whether fault can be attributed to the corporation at all.

As noted in chapter 5, the concept of "genuine" corporate intent or blameworthiness has not merited much attention in general theories of corporate liability. Instead, the development of corporate criminal liability has been the product of a general desire to exert state control over increasing corporate power.[8] The doctrine of vicarious responsibility, adopted from *respondeat superior* in the law of torts, is the common rule of law in the federal courts and allows corporations to be held accountable for the acts of the individuals within the corporation if the agent commits the crime within the scope of his employment with the express purpose of benefiting the corporation. Such a doctrine violates the principles of desert, as there is little in this position that reflects genuine corporate blameworthiness.

... The Model Penal Code offers an array of corporate-liability systems that comes closer to reflecting corporate intent. Most important, the code proffers a system of liability that is more specific than the doctrine of *respondeat superior* and that attempts to define the will of the corporation at the structural level, where management decisions are made. Thus, a corporation can be held liable for a crime committed by an agent in a high managerial position having "duties of such responsibility that his conduct may be fairly assumed to represent the policy of the corporation."[9]

Although such a system comes closer to establishing genuine corporate blame, culpable actions taken by directors or managers do not by themselves imply that the corporation per se is blameworthy. A more appropriate system of liability from a

... desert perspective is one that places less emphasis on the particular hierarchical position of the actors involved than on the corporation's practices and procedures, or what Peter French refers to as the corporation's "internal decision structure."[10] When an illegal act can be traced through a formal or informal organizational structure representing the decision-making channels of the corporation, and when that act is related in some positive way to the procedural rules or operating policy of the corporation, then the act can be said to be a truly corporate act for which the organization may be held responsible. Furthermore, the degree to which the act is represented in these two components indicates the degree of blameworthiness for the act and may be used as a guide in the sentencing process. To understand how this might be done, it is important to examine the concept of corporate internal decision structures more closely.

Corporate Internal Decision Structures and the Assessment of Blame

According to French, the corporate internal decision (CID) structure can be represented by an organizational, or responsibility, flowchart that indicates stations and levels within the corporate power structure, as well as by corporate decision-recognition rules that entail both procedural rules and policies. When the CID structure is operating properly, it "accomplishes a subordination and synthesis of the intentions and acts of various biological persons into a corporate decision."[11]

Organizational Flowchart   The purpose of an organizational flowchart is to identify a corporation's managerial levels and departments and to delineate their responsibility and hierarchical dependence within the corporation. The chart clarifies channels of communication and ensures that the actions and policies taken are, in fact, corporate policies. In doing so, the chart distinguishes the points within the corporation where credit or blame may be imposed for corporate actions.[12]

Reliance on a formal organizational flowchart is open to the criticism that such a chart fails to represent the "real" manner in which decisions are made. Critics maintain that decision-making channels are informal, and structured or weighted in a fashion that is entirely different from those on the formal charts. Perhaps no formal charts exist at all. Yet, as French has noted, an informal decision-making structure may make locating responsibility more complicated, but it does not render the premise underlying flow-charts meaningless. Where the structure is informal, one would be required to piece together the corporate decision-making process on the basis of information provided by individuals within the corporation who are familiar with this informal decision-making process.

Procedural Rules   Understanding the corporation's flowchart is a first step in assigning corporate responsibility for illegal actions. Another vital component of any corporation's CID structure is the set of rules governing the corporation's activity—its procedural rules. Borrowing from H. L. A. Hart, French states that one can determine whether a corporation's decision was made for corporate reasons by examining the procedural rules of the decision-making process and the policies that guide the choice of action.[13] Procedural rules not only establish, but also represent, the chain of decision making and the channels of authority in the corporate structure. These rules may be determined, in part, by the flowchart of corporate activities. The rules may also be determined by examining such things as memoranda about basic production, marketing, and financial planning strategies.

The importance of procedural rules in locating responsibility is illustrated in the recent Union Carbide debate over the jurisdiction of damage claims for the deaths and injuries to residents of Bhopal, India, caused by the leak of methyl isocyanate from a Union Carbide pesticide plant there. According to the corporation, the decisions surrounding the operations of the plant, as well as the decisions made in response to the gas leak, did not represent Union Carbide Corporation of America, but rather were the decisions of Union Carbide India, Ltd. An official at the corporation's Connecticut headquarters stated:

> We would like to note that Union Carbide Corporation does not control Union Carbide India, Ltd., ... The Indian subsidiary is

Culpability and Seriousness

a separate and independent legal entity incorporated in India, managed and operated exclusively by Indian citizens in India. [It] operates under the directions of its board of directors, who are responsible to its more than 23,000 stockholders. [14]

In response to this claim, Indian officials have produced hundreds of internal documents—including Union Carbide position papers, memos, and telexes, representing the procedural rules of the American corporation—to demonstrate that Union Carbide did have control over the operations of the Indian subsidiary. Among the pieces of evidence supporting Union Carbide India, Ltd. (UCIL): (1) a memo signed by Union Carbide Corporation (UCC) Chief Executive Officer Warren M. Anderson authorizing a plan to sell or write down assets of UCIL seven months prior to the leak; (2) a memo demonstrating a conflict between U.S. officials and the UCIL board of directors over misjudged costs of production and demand for the agricultural products produced at the Bhopal plant showing opposition by the board to future investment at Bhopal; and (3) a document signed by Warren Anderson and other top company officials approving a plan in May 1984 to reduce UCC's equity stake in its Indian subsidiary to 40 percent, from its level at that time of 50.9 percent. [15]

It is often true that procedural rules are not always easily located. In part this is because of the complexity of large-scale corporations, where size, delegation of duties, and increased specialization combine to create "an institutionalization of irresponsibility." [16] Some corporate legal scholars have also argued that procedural rules are purposefully neglected by corporations that engage in illegal behavior. This minimization of procedural rules thereby enables higher management to veil itself in intentional ignorance. Managers point to the wide discretion granted to lower-level agents to carry on certain activities and to make decisions on their own.

However, although explicit procedural rules may often be kept to a minimum, corporations *must* have these rules in order to survive day to day. As French notes, even in free-form corporate decision structures where discretion exists

> official or station duties are usually clearly defined, and the appearance of wide discretion is only a disguise for implicit procedural structure. The notions 'within one's authority' and 'exceeding one's authority' are almost always clearly defined, at least in daily operation.[17]

Policy Rules While procedural rules represent the chain of corporate decision making, policy rules represent the corporation's operating guides or principles. Peter Drucker has noted that every corporation has a set of operating guides that serve as its policy statement:

> Because the corporation is an institution it must have a basic policy. For it must subordinate individual ambitions and decisions to the *needs* of the corporation's welfare and survival. That means that it must have a set of principles and a rule of conduct which limit and direct individual actions and behaviors.[18]

French terms this set of principles the policy "recognitors" of the corporation. As with procedural rules, policy rules again may be determined by looking at the operational documents and written policies of the corporation. Such sources include annual reports, codes and policies for corporate employees, and memoranda that define the corporation's business principles. These sources may be formal or informal. Furthermore, they can be said to represent the goals and objectives of the corporation, the appropriate means by which those goals and objectives are to be achieved, and the image the corporation wishes to portray to those working within it, as well as to those in the outside world.[19]

Culpability and Seriousness

The use of policy rules in locating blame is well illustrated in a case brought against Sharp Corporation.[20] In 1975, Sharp Australia, a subsidiary of the multinational Japan-based Sharp Corporation, was prosecuted on ten charges of blatantly misleading advertising in violation of the provisions of the 1974 Trade Practices Act. According to the judge in the case, the Australian subsidiary's misleading advertising was not the product of carelessness but rather contained "the marks of too much construction." "Sharp's failure was a failure to involve the appropriate technically qualified people in checking advertising copy before publication."[21] Perhaps more revealing were the comments of one of the solicitors representing Sharp:

> An administration was allowed to evolve which was heavy on selling talent but which saw advertising only as a selling tool and not as an administrative responsibility. Accurate records were not kept of key meetings, a vital letter was completely mislaid, the technical department was clearly never in proper liaison with the advertising department.[22]

In an effort to remedy the problems and prevent the likelihood of future occurrences, Sharp not only revised its advertising policies but also introduced a checking procedure into the corporate process.

> All advertising material became subject to mandatory review by technical staff, several of whom are now stationed in the marketing section; this integration of technical and marketing functions was aimed specifically at avoiding the type of communication breakdown which led to the 1975 offenses.[23]

Cases other than the Union Carbide and Sharp examples demonstrate how an analysis of the CID structure can be used to locate corporate responsibility.

In September 1985 American Airlines paid a $1.5 million fine (the largest in aviation history) to the Federal Aviation Administration after being cited for a series of maintenance-related violations. Twenty-six infractions were alleged, ranging from flying airplanes that were not airworthy to using unacceptable plastic parts. Most serious were the charges that the airline failed to report all its maintenance problems and that it delayed repairs even after its pilots complained. An analysis of the CID structure by the FAA produced evidence that the corporation's procedural rules regarding maintenance and safety-related issues were systematically ignored. Evidence was also presented concerning the maintenance practices of the airline. American suffered from a severe shortage of mechanics and consistently encountered delays in both repairs and inspections. These troublesome maintenance practices were especially significant in light of the FAA's examination of the overall policies of American Airlines. At the time of the violations, American Airlines was in the midst of a large expansion effort. According to a report in the *Wall Street Journal*:

> FAA officials blamed most of American's maintenance problems on the airline's aggressive expansion efforts. In particular, the officials faulted the carrier for not deploying maintenance people in some cities where it started offering service. That forced American to improperly defer maintenance. . . . In some cases . . . the airline had pilots making maintenance-related decisions they were unqualified to make. "Their problem was a lack of adequate planning for maintenance," said one FAA official.[24]

In American Airlines' corporate policy, expansion efforts outweighed maintenance plans in such a way as to reduce the safety margins expected of air carriers. While company officials denied that pilots were making decisions that they were unqualified to make, they did announce plans to hire 550 new employees and stated that the company had made changes in its maintenance and inspection procedures.[25]

A faulty CID structure was also evident in the criminal conviction of E. F. Hutton and Company. Two thousand counts of fraud related to overdrafting were brought against the firm. No charges were lodged against individual agents of the company.[26]

Public records of the Hutton case point out how the formal and informal corporate internal decision structures, and companies' procedures and policies, can be used to verify the "corporateness" of an illegal act upon which blame may be imposed. Hutton was accused of systematically overdrafting checks as they moved from branch offices to central accounts and of manipulating the "float" time during which checks were cleared. Both actions allowed the company to obtain hundreds of millions of dollars of interest-free loans.

An examination of the company's organizational chart (in combination with its procedural and policy rules) demonstrates the corporate nature of the overdraft process. According to the Justice Department, twenty-four individuals and thirty Hutton branch offices engaged in the systematic "drawdown" of accounts between July 1980 and February 1982. Although Hutton executives denied knowledge of the activity, company records and internal memoranda indicate that the senior management was aware of the process and apparently authorized it. For example, two memos were written by Hutton's comptroller to the president of the company; one, "Interest on Regional Bank Overdrafting," acknowledged the president's comments concerning the process. According to one account:

> The two page document first notes that [the president] made the decision to give branches credit from interest earned via overdrafting of regional bank accounts. Then it outlines a series of detailed recommendations about how millions of dollars of such profits should be "determined and accounted for," as they are distributed within the firm.
>
> Another section of the two-page memo asserts that certain calculations were "made by asking the regions which bank accounts

they were using to overdraft the branches." A copy also was supposed to go to the unit's senior vice president for corporate development at the time.

In March, [the comptroller] sent a follow-up memo to Hutton's
branch managers, regional officials and a number of senior executives at headquarters outlining procedures for dividing profits
generated from regional overdrafts. The memo indicates [the pres-
ident] was sent a copy as well, along with . . . the executive vice
president of the unit and . . . also to one of the firm's primary
cash-management officials and . . . to a senior vice president of the
brokerage house.[27]

The corporate nature of check overdrafting was apparent not
only in the company's procedures but in its policy as well, albeit
in a more informal fashion. According to the *Wall Street Journal*, the "practices were considered legal and were consistent
with the approved company policy." Further,

former Hutton officials . . . recalled that in many company offices
during those years it was common knowledge that repeated overdrafts were used to manipulate the check-clearing system. "Everyone talked about manipulating the float, from senior management
on down," maintained a former company official who claims some
suspect practices continued well into 1983. "It was kind of an open
secret."[28]

Another of the company's branch managers states that the
overdrafting he engaged in "had been promoted by company
management and was part of corporate cash management." He
added that Hutton's senior management was "certainly making us aware of opportunities" to increase profits by excessive
overdrafting.[29] Finally, it was also apparent that the policy of
overdrafting continued in spite of complaints by banks over the
procedure:

During the summer of 1981, one of Hutton's larger accounts, at
Chemical Bank, was "uncollected 34 of 38 business days." . . . A
bank staff memo to a vice president in New York accused Hutton of
"flagrantly abusing its relationship" with the bank by consistently

writing checks on uncollected balances and by running up more than $112 million in overdrafts on a single day.[30]

DETERMINING LEVELS OF INTENT

Given that liability can be established by examining CID structures, how can this process be used to establish specific levels of intent for the purpose of punishment? And how can this process be used to distinguish the different levels in a way meaningful for sentencing?

Using the four grades of culpability—purpose, knowledge, recklessness, and negligence—as guides, a corporation can be said to act *purposefully* when its flowchart and/or procedural rules and policies (formal or informal) reflect an objective to engage in the illegal act. In the E. F. Hutton fraud case, the company's procedures (as outlined in the corporate memo from the comptroller to the president), as well as the informal understanding of the acceptability of manipulating the check-clearing system to generate interest-free capital, serve as evidence that corporate activities were *directed* for the expressed intention of generating this illicit income. Where evidence that the corporation acted purposefully can be established, the corporation merits the highest degree of blame, and, if harm is held constant, would receive the most severe punishment.

A corporation is said to act *knowingly* with regard to an offense when the corporate policies, procedures, and practices acknowledge the harmful nature of the activity, or of the circumstances surrounding it, and reflect a recognition of the imminent danger or practical certainty of the harm taking place. Knowledge differs from purpose in that policies and practices demonstrate an indifference to the actual outcome of the act, regardless of whether that outcome is the objective of the act.

Just Deserts for Corporate Criminals

For example, suppose a drug manufacturer studying the effectiveness of a new medication receives reports from testing physicians that virtually all trial patients have suffered extensive debilitating side effects. The corporation ignores the evidence, falsifies testing results to the Food and Drug Administration, and proceeds to market the drug. Within six weeks, 80 percent of consumers report side effects similar to those reported by the trial patients. Unlike the case of purposeful action, it was not the specific objective of the drug company to physically harm those individuals, although the corporation was aware of the imminent likelihood that the harm would take place. If for some miraculous reason none of the consumers reported ailments, the corporation may well have been surprised at the outcome, but it would not have been disappointed.

How can evidence of knowledge be located in terms of the corporation's internal decision structure? While it is unlikely that the flowchart or formal operating guide will produce evidence linking the firm to the offense, an examination of the process of communicating the negative test results within the organization and the reactions to those results will likely reveal much about the *mens rea* of the corporation. A good example is the thalidomide case of the 1950s, which resulted in the death or disfigurement of thousands of children born to mothers taking the medication. In an excellent summary, John Braithwaite cites internal memoranda from one marketing company concerning publication of the risks of peripheral neuritis associated with the drug:

> Distillers bought the license to market thalidomide in Great Britain. The company was primarily a huge spirits and liquor manufacturer. Knowledge of side effects from thalidomide came later to Distillers' attention than [it had] with Grunenthal. But when an awareness did begin, it was suppressed, just as in the case of Gru-

nenthal. By February 1961 dozens of cases of peripheral neuritis had been brought to Distillers' attention. The company began to consider putting "a little more emphasis" on the risk of peripheral neuritis, "in the hope the number of cases will diminish if doctors are aware of the possibility". Distillers' sales people were not altogether enthusiastic about this idea. One sales executive, J. Paton, wrote: "It is not our job to educate the medical profession how to look out for various conditions. From a sales promotion point of view, the more we write on this side effect, the more it is likely to get out of perspective." So the sales people were instructed, "[The] possible occurrence of peripheral neuritis is a remote one and in no way detracts from the main selling point of Distaval: . . . It has a toxic effect of which you should be aware . . . but there is no need to alarm the medical profession or discuss the matter unless it is raised."[31]

The documents presented as evidence demonstrate that the corporation had knowledge of the side effects of the drug and acted, both formally and informally, to hide the ill effects from those who relied on such information the most—the medical profession. The evidence also demonstrates that the corporation continued to sell the product despite the virtual certainty of damaging consequences of the drug.

A corporation acts *recklessly* with regard to an offense when the internal decision structure demonstrates indifference to the danger of the harm that may result. As Hyman Gross so clearly points out, the difference between this degree of culpability and that of knowledge and/or purpose is understood as one affecting the likelihood of escape from the harm. Whereas in an act engaged in knowingly the indifference lies in the virtual certainty of harm actually taking place, the indifference in recklessness lies in the *threat* of the harm.[32]

Suppose a corporation is confronted with the dilemma of where to dispose of the toxic by-products of its activity. The plant is located in a rural area, isolated from any immediate human habitation. In an effort to restrain costs, managers decide against hiring a toxic-waste-disposal company and in favor of burying the by-products in an adjacent field. In the process, no effort is made to determine the level of the water table surrounding the plant, or to examine the extent to which the water is used for human consumption. Although the corporation was aware of the toxicity of the by-products, and the general harm that could occur if they were consumed, the corporation did not consider human use to be a concern. Given the decision-making process and the policies enacted, the corporation could, therefore, be characterized as being indifferent to the risk of danger that accompanies the dumping of toxic chemicals.

Evidence of the recklessness of the conduct could be gleaned from the toxicity reports prepared as a part of the general occupational-safety recording process. Evidence of the conscious indifference to the risk of harm could be obtained by examining the formal and informal decision-making process—the extent to which concerns about the spread of toxic materials were discussed and examined by corporate officials, the consideration of alternative dumping procedures, and the existence or lack thereof of any precautions ordered or conducted in the process of dumping the by-products.

Finally, a corporation can be said to be *negligent* in the commission of an offense when there is evidence from its internal decision structure that it failed to take satisfactory precautions to protect against harmful activity in light of the recognized dangers associated with the activity.

The distinction between negligence and the recklessness can be illustrated by using the toxic-waste-disposal case cited above. In the case of recklessness, the policies of the hypothetical corporation suggest a recognition of the substantial risk of harm associated with the disposal of the by-product and a conscious disregard of this risk by dumping it in the adjacent field. Suppose, however, that the corporation hires an outside firm to

dispose of the waste. Written memoranda and agendas from
meetings demonstrate that the outside company is to be in
charge of the entire operation, and that the timetable and procedures were discussed in detail. Nowhere in the discussion,
however, does the corporation raise questions concerning the
dangers of the toxic materials and the safety procedures to be
used. Here, the decision-making process suggests the corporation's negligence in failing to ensure that the company hired
to dispose of the toxic material would take the precautions
necessary to dump it safely. Whereas in the first instance the
corporation was aware of the possibility of harm and demonstrated an indifference to that risk, in the second instance precautions that should have been considered were not discussed.
The corporation is negligent to the extent that it had an obligation, given the potential harmfulness of the activity, to be certain that adequate safety procedures would be followed.

Again, the corporate quality of the negligent act lies in the
internal decision structure, where the solicitation and review
of the disposal operation were products not of a single actor's
choice, but of the normal operating and decision-making policies of the corporation.

In the above levels of culpability (purpose, knowledge, recklessness, and negligence), the corporation merits descending
levels of punishment (holding harm constant) by virtue of the
reduced blameworthiness associated with the act.

ASSESSING BLAME FOR INDIVIDUAL AGENTS

In recent years, much of the effort to prevent corporate crime
has focused on the individual agents acting within the firm.
Individual liability has gathered widespread support, largely
because of the deterrent and preventative effects it supposedly
lends to the overall enforcement effort.[33] Not surprisingly, the

same utilitarian crime-control rationales have been used in the past to determine the length and type of sentence given to individual offenders. Yet, the nature of corporate crime and the roles individual agents play within the corporation involved in crime raise some important questions for a system of punishment based on desert.

Criminal liability may now be imposed on individuals within a corporation who physically perform the criminal activity (direct actors) as well as on individuals who occupy managerial positions and who authorize the crime (indirect actors). While the "corporate" nature of corporate crime raises some interesting issues concerning motive and circumstances of direct actors that may be applicable as extenuations for sentence, establishing the minimum standards of fault is relatively straightforward. Again, while existing statutes often are vague or confusing with respect to intent requirements for direct actors, sentencing guidelines can adopt the Model Penal Code standards of purpose, knowledge, recklessness, and negligence and then scale the punishments accordingly as a first step.

.. Imposing blame on indirect actors creates more problems in the sentencing process. Clearly, those who authorize the criminal act, in spite of their own physical distance from the offense or the specific knowledge they have of the details of the offense, merit blame for that crime. In the past, the intent standard for indirect actors has largely been governed by the degree of intent required by the provisions to convict direct actors. Section 18 of the U.S. Code. (2[b]) states, for instance, that an indirect actor is criminally liable if, "acting with the state of mind required for the commission of the offense, he causes the other person to engage in the conduct that would constitute an offense if engaged in personally by the defendant." Yet, if punishments are to be scaled according to the gravity of the conduct, there must be a greater understanding of the type of conduct required of indirect agents.

According to one commentary on criminal liability for cor- ••• porate agents, the requirement of specific intent (purpose or knowledge) is satisfied when a managerial officer *commands* or *authorizes* a subordinate to engage in a criminal activity, regardless of whether or not the supervisor was physically involved in the actual crime.[34] This authorization can be direct, as in a stated command to commit the illegal act, or it can be inferred by suggesting that the subordinate do whatever is necessary to achieve a certain goal.

Specific intent has also been satisfied in some cases where ••• the superior knew of the illegal activity and made no effort to prevent it, even though the superior had the power to do so:

> Acquiescence differs from authorization only in that the latter generally refers to an official's explicit approval of an illegal act, while the former simply indicates that the official tolerated its commission. When an employee is aware that his superior knows of his illegal conduct but has not acted to curtail it, acquiescence may be tantamount to silent authorization since the employee can reasonably construe his superior's silence as encouragement to continue.[35]

While the concept of acquiescence can be defended on grounds of deterrence, it is also merited on grounds of desert. An individual in a position to control illegal behavior who fails to do so merits punishment because, without his acquiescence, the crime could not have been committed. Thus, the superior officer of the corporation is doing much more than simply failing to act; rather, he "knowingly permits his authority to be used in the commission of a crime."[36]

On first blush, scaling culpability for corporate agents on the basis of command, authorization, or acquiescence makes sense. Yet, the nature of corporate structure and management

135

raises important concerns about how much blame one can realistically impose on corporate officers for the actions of their subordinates. The literature on corporate crime abounds with critiques on the scope of control of key individual agents of large corporations.[37] As Stone notes, a genuine problem exists in determining the amount of knowledge that those on the top have about the actions of their subordinates:

•• For the most part, men at the highest levels will be involved almost to the full extent of their day with major investment and financial decisions, personnel and budget matters and long-range policy planning. Insofar as they are concerned with operations, they serve not as institutors or implementors of policy, but as reviewers, mediating claims and proposals that arise from lower corporate levels. Such a function does not acquaint them with day to day detail on pollution emission controls, product data design, and the like.[38]

Likewise, as such management and organizational theorists as Herbert A. Simon and Fred Luthans have pointed out, flaws in certain organizational processes (such as the internal control system and communication channels) make the ascription of blame for corporate crimes to individual agents problematic.[39] These difficulties are clearly demonstrated in another commentary on the role of institutional rehabilitation in sentencing:

Large companies have an inherent organizational complexity that tends to diffuse and to obscure individual responsibility for corporate actions. Two related corporate processes play a particularly crucial role in this diffusion. Internal control systems aim to ensure that plans established by senior officials are carried out according to instructions, while internal communication systems are designed in part to ensure that information about the implementation of programs returns to the planners. . . . The delegation of decisional or supervisory duties from higher management downward through several levels and outward across several divisions may fail to account for certain necessary responsibilities, while the transmission of information back up through an equally complex hierarchy may fail to provide adequate processing of potentially critical information by appropriate officials.[40]

Reckless Supervision

Given these difficulties, the ability to establish an agent's intent to authorize criminal activity is suspect. One way around this problem is to incorporate a "reckless supervision" standard in the sentencing guides, as was done by the Senate in 1978 in the revised federal criminal code as it applies to substantive liability claims.[41] This standard could easily be used to scale the gravity of culpability in sentencing as well. The reckless-supervision standard places a lesser degree of blame "for a person responsible for supervising particular activities on behalf of an organization" who contributes to the commission of an offense "by his reckless failure to supervise adequately those activities."[42] To this extent recklessness involves the conscious disregard of a substantial risk of harm, where such disregard constitutes "a gross deviation from the standard of care that a reasonable person would exercise in such a situation."[43] Incorporating such a standard into the sentencing process properly considers the organizational dynamics that affect how persons interact within complex large corporations.

More research is needed in this area to specify how such organizational dynamics come into play and how they may be incorporated in sentencing. For example, many commentators have pointed out that those in high management positions often isolate themselves intentionally from the activities of middle management so as to insulate themselves from criminal responsibility for wrongdoing.[44] In such situations there is clearly little that can be done to demonstrate that blame ought to be imposed as merited. While such issues require more attention from a sentencing commission, the guides considered here provide a good starting point by which individual

Just Deserts for Corporate Criminals

culpability may be assessed for the purpose of establishing and scaling offense seriousness.

AGGRAVATING AND MITIGATING CIRCUMSTANCES FOR CORPORATIONS

Assessing the seriousness of corporate crimes is first directed toward the scaling of harms and culpability in typical offenses. Yet, circumstances often arise that aggravate or mitigate the reprehensibility of conduct in specific instances. A desert-based sentencing system for corporate offenses must therefore consider these factors in a systematic fashion. Two elements will be examined here: the corporation's reactions to an offense and its prior record.

Reactive Policy

Brent Fisse has suggested that corporate culpability should not be limited to fault at the time of the *actus reus* of the offense, but should also consider the performance of the corporation *in reaction* to the offense.[45] He proposes the establishment of a doctrine of reactive corporate fault based on the responsive steps taken by the corporation to correct the policies and practices that allowed the act to occur.[46] The reason for doing so lies in the nature of organizational behavior:

> The concept of reactive *mens rea* reflects very sharply the organizational reality of management by exception. An axiom of orthodox management is that routine tasks should be delegated, leaving managers to use their creativity and leadership to the greatest possible corporate advantage. In the normal course of corporate business, top management assumes that compliance with the law is routine. Management typically issues policy directives from time to time which are implemented by means of standard operating procedures. Only when an "exceptional" event occurs, as when the corporation is alleged to have committed an offense, are questions of compliance referred upwards to managers.[47]

Culpability and Seriousness

Focusing on a corporation's reactive policies is not new in the realm of sentencing. Since many courts use vicarious liability to determine corporate responsibility, they often consider the reactions of the corporation to the offense as possible mitigations to the sentence:

> At sentencing, the court can inquire into developments since the time of the crime and even since the time of the trial. Have new measures been taken to prevent repetition? Have responsible or negligent employees been disciplined or fired? Such a wider angle of vision creates a stronger incentive for the corporation to reform itself.[48]

According to most rationales for punishment, including desert, a corporation's reactions to an offense can be important in sentencing. Clearly, they affect the degree to which a company can be said to be blameworthy for the offense in question. This is particularly true in cases where uncertainty or inconsistency arises within a corporation's internal decision structure. Suppose, for example, a corporation maintains as part of its stated policy that unethical conduct is expressly forbidden and that such conduct is to be considered nonreflective of the corporation's aims and procedures. At the same time evidence reveals that the criminal act in question was authorized by those in the appropriate decision-making channels and even became an informal policy practice. Where such contradictory evidence is presented, the reactive steps taken by the corporation can be considered as evidence that either corroborates or refutes the corporation's supposed policy of law-abidingness. A corporation that quickly implements safety standards, punishes employees associated with the actions, and corrects faulty policy, equipment, or channels of communication appears to demonstrate a compliant corporate policy toward law-abiding behavior and would thus be less at fault than a corporation that takes no steps to remedy its policies and practices and that demonstrates a noncompliant corporate policy.

Prior Record

··· Among desert theorists, the role that a corporation's past history plays in the sentencing process is subject to considerable
· debate. Both Richard Singer and George Fletcher argue that an offender's punishment can be imposed only for that offender's instant offense.[49] Increasing punishment on the basis of prior convictions constitutes double retribution; the offender has already been punished for his past actions and consequently deserves no further punishment for those misdeeds.

· Andrew von Hirsch, on the other hand, has maintained that one's previous criminal acts do have bearing on the punishment given for the instant offense, albeit a lesser bearing than the harm and culpability of the present crime.[50] Before we can address the propriety of considering prior record in the punishment of corporations and their agents it is important to outline von Hirsch's argument in more detail.

Von Hirsch notes that punishment does two things. First, it
··· declares the wrongfulness of the offender's *act*. Second, it expresses disapproval of the *offender himself*.[51] It is this latter aspect that makes prior misconduct relevant to what the person deserves. When an offender comes before the court for the first time, his act represents, at least formally, a departure from his past law-abiding behavior. A first offender may plead that
· his crime represents "a first misstep which was out of keeping with what otherwise had been his practice."[52] Although the offender still deserves punishment for the harm caused by the act, the disapproval should be "dampened" because his actions were atypical of his past behavior.

Von Hirsch suggests several reasons that first offenders
· merit less disapproval than those who have engaged in prior misconduct.[53] The first is that people are at times subject to moments of weakness or willfulness. "We wish to condemn the person for his act, but accord some respect for the fact that his

inhibitions against wrongdoing have functioned on previous occasions, and show some sympathy for the all-too-human frailty that can lead someone to a lapse."[54]

Second, giving the first offender less than the full weight of the criminal sanction provides him with "another chance." The assumption is that since this offense is out of line with previous character, the punishment imposed allows the offender to reconsider his actions and to take seriously their impropriety. In doing so, the criminal law treats the offender as a moral agent.

Third, giving the offender reduced blame incorporates the notion of tolerance in the criminal law—tolerance based on human fallibility and "exposure to pressures and temptations."[55] As the actor continues his misconduct, that tolerance is rightly taken away. The offender demonstrates that he is not concerned with the censure given him for his past actions and that his deeds are not the product of fallibility and weakness, but of a conscious desire to do harm.

While the notion of fallibility makes sense with regard to individual agents acting within a corporation, the application of these principles to corporations is questionable. There is a limit to which corporations may be considered moral actors subject to frailty. Undoubtedly, corporations do have a pattern of behavior that reflects certain ethical preferences—as demonstrated by past actions, standard operating procedures, and policies. It is also true that corporations may engage in activity that is "uncharacteristic" in this regard. Yet, the concepts von Hirsch suggests are ones that describe uncontrollability, a lack of deliberation, and uncertainty—all features that make sense with regard to humans but not to corporations as entities. Corporations are designed, after all, to reduce uncertainty, to maximize control, to optimize deliberation. They are not moral actors in the sense that von Hirsch speaks of, occasionally stumbling because of a lapse of moral strength over which they seemingly have little control.

This does not mean, however, that prior record is not applicable to corporations in the assessment of culpability. It was stated earlier that a corporation's compliance with the rules of the law is reflected in its corporate policies and practices. Because of the complexity suggested earlier of establishing corporate *mens rea* based on corporate structure, practices, procedures, and policies, a corporation's prior record can be used as further evidence to demonstrate its degree of compliance or noncompliance with the law. If, for example, a corporation makes the claim that an offense did not reflect its policies and practices, yet its records indicate previous civil or criminal convictions, warnings, or disciplinary actions, then one could suspect that the corporation's policies and practices are, in fact, noncompliant.

From this perspective, prior record is not per se a basis for greater punishment, but is rather to be used as evidence to establish the degree of culpability for the *current* offense. Thus, prior record becomes one of many items of evidence, including the corporation's reactive policies to the offense, to be considered as aggravating or mitigating criteria in sentencing.

AGGRAVATING AND MITIGATING CIRCUMSTANCES FOR INDIVIDUALS

So far the concern here has been limited to the general ratings of seriousness to be given to individual agents with reference to their culpability—for instance, the conditions that determine whether one acts purposely, knowingly, recklessly, or negligently and that may be incorporated in the sentencing guidelines. There are, however, a number of factors that merit consideration as aggravating or mitigating circumstances in sentencing the individual. Such elements as excuses (necessity or duress, for example) and the offender's motives merit further consideration in terms of their application to the sentencing decision, since it is clear that they affect the defendant's culpability in some fashion.[56] Although greater attention must be paid to these concerns with regard to corporate crime, two factors, ignorance of the law and the actor's degree of involvement, stand out as issues meriting consideration as aggravating or mitigating factors in the sentencing of individual agents.

Ignorance of the Law

The extent of the offender's knowledge of the illegality of his conduct appears relevant as a mitigating factor in punishment. While ignorance of the law has not been a defense with common crimes, it merits consideration for corporate agents, if only at sentencing, because of the complexity of the laws regulating corporate conduct.[57] Control of corporate conduct is attempted through myriad rules and regulations that are often times vague and confusing and are under constant revision. Given the dynamic nature of corporate regulations, many agents find themselves relying on the advice of corporate counsel about the propriety of certain conduct. This defense, while justifiably to be considered as a factor mitigating the degree of blame one can impose on a single individual, must entail certain qualifications, however.

The issue here is not simply complexity of the law or reliance on corporate counsel, but rather the care the person took in ascertaining the essential facts of the law. Given the complexity of the law, did the individual take the necessary steps to understand the full implications of the law and the requirements or restrictions imposed on him by virtue of that law? Where the

143

agent exercised caution, sought advice, and made efforts to understand the law, his actions reflect a reduced level of culpability that may readily be adopted as a mitigating factor in sentencing.

Actor's Degree of Involvement

As mentioned earlier, individuals often find themselves participants in a particular criminal activity that involves a large number of others who are directly or indirectly associated with the crime. The degree and importance of that involvement may also be factors in considering aggravation or mitigation—not in terms of the duress that the individual may feel as a result of being "caught" in the middle of the activity, but in terms of the vitality of the offender's own involvement. For instance, the lab assistant who is ordered to destroy negative test results seems less culpable than the lab director who gave the order, and who further presented erroneous positive data to the unit manager, knowing they would be used to recommend that the product be placed on the market. The lab director, on the other hand, seems less culpable than the unit manager who repeatedly disregarded complaints from a variety of sources and who ordered a number of subordinates to falsify data regarding the product to present a comprehensive picture of product effectiveness. The degree to which an individual's activity encouraged the commission of the offense, or could have prevented the offense, undoubtedly affects the degree to which he or she can be blamed for the occurrence or the risk of the offense.

CONCLUSION

Culpability in the corporate context is a complex issue. Desert-based sentencing systems, more so than deterrence-based systems, place it in a crucial role. Determining culpability for the purposes of assessing seriousness in sentencing is made more difficult by the fact that the substantive corporate law concerning liability is grounded so comprehensively in deterrence concerns. It is difficult, therefore, to readily incorporate in the sentencing context the principles concerning liability in the substantive law. It makes little intuitive sense to scale the gravity of offenses for the purposes of sentencing by incorporating culpability considerations when the offense is one for which strict liability is imposed. Nor can one realistically alter the severity of the punishment according to the same principle of vicarious responsibility that established guilt. Such notions are incorporated to foster deterrence aims. They are simply incompatible with the principles of desert.

Given this point, a truly workable desert-based sentencing system could be developed more easily if changes were made in the substantive law as well. Yet, the sentencing system *can* be made to reflect desert concerns without requiring major revisions in the substantive law as a first step. It has been suggested here that culpability—for the purposes of punishing both corporations as entities and individual agents acting on behalf of the corporation—be scaled first according to degrees of fault as established in the Model Penal Code. The factors used to establish those degrees of fault can be determined by examining the organizational internal decision structure, if the offender is the corporation, and the knowledge and level of participation in the offense, if the offender is the individual.

More research is necessary in the area of corporate and personal culpability for corporate crimes as it relates to issues in sentencing. Much can be learned from case studies (as well as from organizational theory) about the channels of responsibility, delegation of authority, and insulation from blame—issues

145

that appear to be common, yet problematic, within corporations. Yet, for the purposes intended here, a realistic scale can be constructed that more clearly considers levels of culpability in the corporate context.

CHAPTER 8

Scaling Punishments for Corporations and Their Agents

TO UNDERSTAND how a desert-based punishment scale may be constructed for corporate offenses, it is important that we first make a clear distinction between what von Hirsch terms the *ordinal* and *cardinal* magnitudes of punishments.[1] The first of these issues, the ordinal magnitude, concerns how crimes should be punished relative to each other. The latter concerns the absolute levels of severity that are used to anchor the punishment scale. Desert is the determining principle in deciding ordinal magnitudes. However, there is no inherent or "natural" punishment that can be said to be deserved for any given crime, and an attempt to establish one would surely be improper. To the extent that desert is useful in determining the cardinal magnitude of a punishment scale, it is as a limiting principle in determining this parameter of punishment severity.[2]

This chapter examines the issues involved in fixing a punishment scale for corporate offenses. In doing so it addresses the propriety of punishment options available for corporations, as well as for individual agents, with respect to the central principles of ordinal and cardinal proportionality. The chapter also examines the applicability of other utilitarian concerns, in particular that of deterrence, in the anchoring of punishments for corporate offenses, as well as the practical issues involved in the sentencing process for such offenses.

ORDINAL AND CARDINAL MAGNITUDES

The ordinal magnitude of a punishment scale concerns the relative severity of different punishments for different offenses. In establishing the ordinal magnitude, proportionality between offense seriousness and punishment severity is the guide. Here, two requirements must be satisfied. The first is
· · *parity*: offenders whose crimes are similar in harm and culpability must be punished with equal severity. The second requirement is *rank ordering*:[3] the punishments established on
· · any scale must be graded in a way that reflects the differences in the relative seriousness of the criminal acts.

The vitality of these requirements lies in the notion of fairness. As stressed earlier, the criminal sanction condemns wrongful conduct. It expresses that condemnation through the punishment imposed for the criminal conduct. Given that punishment is condemnatory, justice requires that offenders be punished according to the blameworthiness of their acts. To treat those involved in similarly reprehensible conduct differently, or to punish for serious offenses more leniently than for less serious offenses, would be to express disproportionate censure and would thus distort the condemnatory implications of punishment, rendering the treatment unjust.[4]

By punishing like offenses alike and by grading sentences according to the comparative seriousness of offenses, ordinal-proportionality requirements are satisfied. Yet, essential to the construction of a punishment scale is the concern for cardinal proportionality; here, anchoring points must be located that "begin to establish the levels of severity appropriate for given degrees of blameworthiness:"[5]

> Even where penalties on a scale have been ranked in the order of crimes' seriousness, the scale may infringe cardinal proportionality if its overall severities are sufficiently inflated or deflated. A scale so inflated that it visits extensive deprivations of liberty on lesser

criminal conduct is objectionable, because it overstates the blame for that conduct or else undervalues the importance of the rights of which the defendant is being deprived. To imprison criminals even for routine thefts would necessitate either treating such acts as more seriously reprehensible than they are; or else treating the defendant's liberty (inappropriately) as so unimportant that its deprivation can serve as an expression of lesser censure. Similar reasoning will support objections to deflating the penalty scale so much that serious crimes are visited with mild punishments.[6]

Desert provides limits, but not specific solutions, to determining the overall magnitude of the punishment scale. Agreement can be reached that a given standard is reasonable or unreasonable as an expression of condemnation through the deprivations it imposes, but it is does not provide any explicit answer such as "price fixing deserves *x* fine for corporations or *x* years in prison for individual agents." Finding some starting point (or anchoring point, as von Hirsch calls it) is necessary.[7] Once an anchoring point has been set, comparative judgments can be made that relate the severity of the punishment to the severity of the offense.

In addressing this issue, von Hirsch focuses on the line, termed the "in-out" line, separating the use of prison and non-prison sanctions. He states that cardinal proportionality delineates a range of punishments that clearly merit imprisonment, and a range of punishments that clearly merit nonprison sanctions. Yet, desert provides no clear answer as to where the in-out line should be drawn between those two bands. Given this inability, other concerns, which include penal resources and some crime-control considerations, may be called on to establish this boundary. Von Hirsch, for instance, explores (albeit cautiously) the possible use of categorical incapacitation.[8]

Above all, the punishment scale must reflect ordinal proportionality by maintaining parity and rank order, and the absolute levels of punishment must fairly reflect its condemnatory implications, in that the scale as a whole is not unduly harsh or unduly lenient *in terms of the reprobation it represents*. This latter concern is, of course, a question of judgment. But that it is a judgment, subject to disagreement about what is overly harsh or overly lenient, does not make it unresolvable. Von Hirsch suggests the possibility of incorporating other crime-control considerations in determining the anchoring points and magnitudes of the scale. Yet, while this approach is useful—given some knowledge of the effects on crime reduction of any given policy—it is only one of several conventions that may be used. One argument can be made for using desert considerations alone to determine the anchoring points and the magnitude of a punishment scale. If one has the criteria by which to determine that any given punishment (what is to be used as an anchoring point), or the entire scale itself, is overly lenient or overly harsh, then it holds that the same criteria may be used to determine what is an appropriate punishment or scale. In other words, if we can determine what is unreasonable we should also be able to determine what is reasonable, at least for establishing the limits, both upper and lower, of the scale. John Kleinig has suggested that one way to accomplish this is to determine, albeit in a normative fashion, the most severe punishment and the most lenient punishment one is willing to impose on offenders.

> It is [these] limits which . . . provide the natural points of contact for our two scales. In relating punishment to offenses, we simply reserve the mildest punishment we can reasonably give for the least serious wrong, the most severe punishment for the most wicked deed and scale other wrongs and punishments in between in accordance with the pattern of scaling (considering parity and rank order) we described earlier. . . . Such a view incorporates both proportionality and equivalence in that the wrong and the punishment occupy the same relative position on their respective scales.[9]

Scaling Punishments

Yet this solution raises some significant concerns as well. Most important, there is no guiding philosophy underlying what is to be considered the severest punishments and the mildest punishments at our disposal. Without more specific limiting principles, the establishment of maximum and minimum levels of punishment will be fickle at best.

Another alternative is to incorporate resource constraints into the scale. Here, prison-population figures and the costs of various punishment options would serve as guides in establishing the absolute levels of the punishment scale. This strategy will be discussed in greater detail later on. Note that choosing the most appropriate convention depends, in part, on the validity of the suggested crime-control strategy and its reliability in achieving its stated goal. This choice also depends on the extent to which the sentencing body implementing the scale wishes to incorporate multiple goals into the sentencing process. This latter concern will likely arise in response to public or political pressures to "get tough" on crime. Finally, whether one chooses to incorporate crime-control strategies or to rely on basic concepts of desert, the costs of punishment will ultimately merit consideration.

ALLOCATING PUNISHMENTS FOR CORPORATE CRIME

Constructing a punishment scale that reflects these desert principles presents some unique concerns with respect to corporate crimes. Most obviously, there is the need for two separate and distinct punishment scales for these offenses—one for corporations, and another for individual agents—because of the different punishments available and appropriate for each.

The first step in examining the issues related to the development of a desert-based punishment scale for corporate offenses is to review the different kinds of sanctions available for both corporations and individuals. In chapter 2 these sanctions were critiqued with respect to their supposed deterrent effectiveness. The intent here is to examine and critique them from the requirements of proportionality outlined above. What will become evident is that most of these sanctions present serious problems with respect to ordinal and cardinal proportionality.

Sanctions against the Corporation

Before examining the different types of punishments available for corporations, a more general question must be addressed: What is a meaningful punishment to be imposed on corporations?

Virtually all definitions of punishment contain as a central component the quality of unpleasantness. Some make reference to hard treatment, while others are quicker to label punishment as what it is—painful treatment. While determining what forms of retribution constitute significant unpleasantness has perhaps always been subject to some debate, nowhere is it more in dispute than when it comes to the punishment of corporations. While no two individuals are alike, it seems a truism that, with rare exceptions, human beings do not differ greatly in their opinions of what constitutes hard treatment. Although sophisticated time-perception studies have not been conducted in prisons, several other reviews probed the general severity of certain forms of punishment. Interestingly, people are fairly consistent in their responses to the severity of certain forms, as well as amounts, of punishment. There seems to be general agreement that incarceration is a significant punishment, at least with reference to its general unpleasantness.

Scaling Punishments

Unlike individuals, however, corporations vary greatly in their capacity to endure hard treatment. This is most obvious when the supposed hard treatment involves a "negative profit contingency." The use of fines will be examined in more detail later in this chapter, yet what is clear is that the significance of the punishment is a very relative notion indeed when the object of the fine is a corporation. This is true in absolute terms, as well as in terms of the specific offense. With respect to the latter, many may question the significance of a fine that constitutes one one-hundreth of the gain from the criminal act. E. F. Hutton's check-kiting scheme, for example, resulted in a monetary gain for the company of somewhere between $4 billion and $10 billion. The fine imposed on the company was $215 million. The significance of such a relatively lenient fine is questionable on both deterrent and desert grounds.

Perhaps more important, with regard to absolute terms, a corporation ranked in the *Fortune* 500 will not incur anything near the degree of unpleasantness (if felt at all) of a criminal fine as the unpleasantness felt by a smaller company receiving the same fine. Determining the cardinal levels of a punishment scale on the basis of the impact of a fine on the wealthiest of all possible victims obviously produces serious concerns for justice. At least from a desert perspective, the punishment or harsh treatment itself reflects the condemnation merited by the criminal act. Assessing cardinal limits on the basis of the unpleasantness incurred by the wealthiest offenders will result in gross overstatements of the censure implied by the fine when the corporation involved is less wealthy. Some solutions to these problems, such as the development of a day-fine system for corporations, will be suggested later in this chapter. Let us now examine the types of punishments currently being proffered and analyze them with respect to the principles of commensurate deserts.

··· *Community Service*   The imposition of community-service provisions as punishment for corporate offenses has received great notoriety over the past several years as a result of its use as a condition of probation in some large corporate-crime cases. [10] Perhaps the two best-known cases involve *United States v. Allied Chemical Corporation* and *United States v. Olin Mathieson Corporation*. [11] In the first case, Allied Chemical was fined $13.24 million on 940 counts of polluting public water with the pesticide Kepone. The judge reduced the fine to $5 million after Allied agreed to establish a research center (the Virginia Environmental Endowment) to study the effects of Kepone, at a cost of $8,356,202. [12]

In the Olin Mathieson case, the firearms manufacturer pleaded no contest to conspiracy to ship weapons to South Africa in violation of a trade embargo. The judge in that case set the fine at $45,000 after the company agreed to establish a "New Haven Community Betterment Fund" with $500,000. [13]

Such sanctions have stirred public controversy. Perhaps the most disturbing argument concerns the corporation's ability to deduct from its taxes the costs of community service in mitigation of fine. [14] In addition, these sanctions have come under attack as allowing for too much judicial discretion. Judges have the option to choose a host of programs, many of which are suggested by the corporations themselves.

Several commentators have called for greater attention to community service as a sentence by itself, as opposed to a condition of probation. [15] Brent Fisse has suggested that such provisions be adopted in Australia. In his model provisions, he defines community-service projects as follows:

(a)   A project of community service shall be either a project proposed by the offender and agreed to by the court or a project specified by the court.

(b)   A project of community service shall have as its object the

154

redress of a social harm occasioned by the offense subject to sentence and the redress sought shall take one or more of the following forms:

(i) direct redress by restoration, specific or approximate, of what has been harmed by the offense;

(ii) substitutionary redress by development or introduction of measures designed to provide better means of preventing or redressing harm of the type proscribed by the offense;

(iii) substitutionary redress by participation in a program of social action authorized by regulation.[16]

Fisse goes on to suggest the following quantitative and temporal limits to community service:

(a) The amount of community service required to be performed shall be quantified in terms of the actual net loss cost of materials, equipment and labor to be used for the project.

(b) Unless provided otherwise the maximum cost of community service under a community service order shall be the same as the maximum amount of the fine or monetary penalty applicable to the offense for which the order is made.

(c) A project of community service shall be performed within two years of the date of sentence unless the court orders otherwise.[17]

Despite the increased favorable attention given to the community-service sanction for corporations, it does have some troubling features. Roger Hood has pointed out the great uncertainty that has surrounded community-service orders for individual offenders convicted of common crimes, and there is reason to believe that similar uncertainty will prevail with respect to corporations as well.[18] Clearly, from a desert perspective, questions must be raised concerning the condemnatory implications of such punishments. Focusing on community service, whether it be specific involvement in a program or a financial donation to a specific cause, runs the risk of turning attention away from the wrongfulness of the conduct and toward some other material benefit that will derive from the criminal activity—mainly, the community program to be created. This point is not to be overstated. Certainly the goal of retributive punishment is not simply to grind one's heel in the face of the offender. Yet, corporations are well versed in image making, and community-service provisions are likely candidates for massive advertising campaigns extolling the virtues of the firm's civic-mindedness. In the midst of all this, it seems probable that the condemnatory impact of punishment will be lost.

As they are now designed, community-service sanctions also raise problems from the standpoint of ordinal proportionality, since the amount of the service to be provided by the corporation is usually unrelated in any real way to the harm of the offense. The model provisions suggested by Fisse tie the amount of the community service to the net cost of materials, equipment, and labor necessary for the specific project imposed. Yet, these tasks are directed toward what the corporation is capable of undertaking and not, per se, to the seriousness of the offense: a drug manufacturer, for instance, may be required to do research on the effects of a certain drug; a manufacturing company may be required to endow a chair at a university to focus on business ethics. Clearly, under such provisions both parity and rank order are in no way protected. Community-service projects differ to such an extent that offenders convicted of like offenses will have very different net costs and thus disproportional punishments.

These reservations do not imply that community-service provisions are inherently unworkable in a system based on principles of desert. To establish a scale of such provisions that meets proportionality requirements, set monetary amounts would need to be determined beforehand that would be imposed equally on all corporate offenders found guilty of the same offense and that would be scaled to reflect the relative seriousness of the offenses. Yet, these requirements may well detract from the original intent of community service—to develop some useful and workable project—since its goal (for example, clean water, a new drug on the market, an information clearinghouse for defective products) has no necessary relationship to set monetary amounts. Thus, community service as a viable punishment merits more research and attention to make it workable from a desert-based perspective.

Structural Intervention   Another relatively new form of punishment involves structural intervention in the operations and management of the corporation itself. For the most part this sanction has been restricted to the civil realm, principally through ancillary remedies in SEC civil-enforcement suits.[19] The purpose of this intervention is to reduce or eliminate those elements in the corporation's process and structure that induce criminal activity. Implementing auditing procedures, improving information-reporting strategies, or entering directly into the corporate process by removing certain personnel or by interjecting new personnel to monitor the company are some of the forms of structural intervention that have been suggested.[20]

While structural intervention merits greater scholarly attention, it is not, as it now stands, an appropriate sanction from a desert-based punishment perspective. As stressed earlier, desert-based punishment differs from utilitarian punishment in that it looks solely to the past offense, not to the likelihood of future misconduct. Yet, structural intervention strives to accomplish precisely the opposite, by eliminating future criminal activity.

One might argue that structural intervention could be tailored to concern itself only with the past practices that caused the criminal activity and thus be more in line with notions of desert. This tailoring might be done, for example, by imposing a fine, based on the seriousness of the offense, and then requiring that structural or procedural changes directly related to the past offense be made (without exceeding the cost of the fine imposed). Such intervention would be similar in a sense to the imposition of a presumptive probation period on an offender, but with the conditions of probation keyed to specific problems that the offender has demonstrated by his criminal conduct.

Even with these modifications, significant problems still loom from a desert perspective. As with community service, structural intervention deemphasizes the condemnatory aspect of punishment. The focus shifts from the reprobative nature of the criminal sanction to the likelihood of rehabilitation.

Concerns for proportionality are again raised with this type of sanction. The impact of structural intervention is difficult to control. Because the consequences, or harshness, of structural interventions are unknown, even the vague boundaries of cardinal proportionality may be threatened by their use.

The most troubling feature of such a sanction does not concern cardinal proportionality, however, but ordinal proportionality. By definition, neither parity nor rank order will exist with structural intervention; different corporations involved in similar offenses are unlikely to act for the same reasons. It is doubtful that they will have equivalent structural or organizational deficiencies that led to the crime. Corporations involved in very serious offenses may require little structural intervention, while others involved in less serious offenses may have great deficiencies in structure and operation and may require the full impact of the sanction available. To force ordinal proportionality criteria into such a sanction would work against it, and would in all likelihood render the sanction meaningless from both rehabilitative and desert standpoints.

Again, it is important to stress that these difficulties should

not be taken as a rejection of this form of regulation. The point
is that structural intervention is unacceptable as a criminal
punishment from a perspective that focuses on the blaming
features of punishment and on the importance of the proportionality of that condemnation. Such a remedy may still be
applicable (given further study of its effects on deterrence)
from a civil standpoint, where the focus lies heavily on regulation, as opposed to condemnation.

Adverse Publicity   Perhaps the sanction receiving the greatest notoriety in recent discussions of corporate punishment is
the formal use of adverse publicity against corporations convicted of illegal activity. In *The Impact of Publicity on Corporate Offenders*, Brent Fisse and John Braithwaite explore the
effects of adverse publicity stemming from involvement in
criminal activity of seventeen large corporations.[21] The authors' findings suggest that although such criticism causes a
negative measurable financial impact on only a few of the corporations studied, virtually all companies felt or strongly
feared some ensuing damage to their *prestige*. The authors
advocate the increased use of formal publicity—court-ordered
publication of the details of the offense—as well as reforms
taken to prevent the activity from occurring again, as one of
perhaps several punishments to be levied against corporate
lawbreakers.

I noted in chapter 2 that this sanction raises questions about
its deterrent effectiveness.[22] It is not at all clear, for example,
that the loss of corporate prestige can be translated into future
law-abiding behavior. While adverse publicity may have promise as a deterrent sanction, much more empirical research
will be needed to test the proposition. More problematic, however, are the concerns such a sanction presents from a desert
perspective.

Just Deserts for Corporate Criminals

It is true that, unlike community service and probation, adverse publicity is strongly tied to the notions of blame and condemnation, and comports therefore with basic notions of retributive punishment. However, when one examines the issues involved in the allocation of punishments, specifically concerning concepts of ordinal and cardinal proportionality, the use of adverse publicity is indeed troubling.

Fisse and Braithwaite acknowledge the uncertainty of the ultimate impact of adverse publicity, yet they discount concerns about proportionality, on the grounds that "[t]he most that is required to satisfy the principle of proportionality is formal proportionate quantification of sentence in advance, irrespective of the actual impact upon an offender."[23]

The determination of punishment severity is not made on an offender-by-offender basis, but rather on judgments of the severity of a certain form or length of punishment in a general sense. Even here, adverse publicity has difficulties. First, unlike a fine or imprisonment, with which one can get some general idea of the consequences of punishment and thereby establish general outer limits on the absolute levels of deserved punishment, prestige reduction caused by adverse publicity is a difficult concept to understand, even in broad terms. Even if limits are placed on the duration of the publicity, the form it is to take, and the cost of the advertising, it is not ultimately time, form, or cost that is important to establish, but some reasonable understanding of the effects on prestige that those components are likely to have. While it may be possible someday to find the range of impact on prestige, and the concurrent results of that impact on other areas of the corporation's life, there is at present insufficient evidence of what this range may entail.[24]

Adverse publicity raises more troubling issues when one is concerned with the requirement of ordinal proportionality.

Again, as the authors point out, all sanctions are likely to affect individual offenders differently, and the only way to ensure proportionality is through some quantification and presumptive format at the outset. Thus, if all offenders convicted of a particular offense were subject, for example, to publicity orders of four full-page magazine advertisements in the same type of magazines at the same cost and at the same time, one could argue that ordinal-proportionality requirements were being satisfied as well as possible, given the nature of the sanction. Yet, adverse-publicity sanctions, at least as suggested by Fisse and Braithwaite, are not intended to be so structured. In fact, the authors argue that adverse publicity is not to be used in all instances, but rather carefully and selectively to maximize its impact.[25] Such use violates parity and, in all probability, rank order as well. For a punishment to satisfy ordinal-proportionality requirements it must be used for all offenders in a given category of offenses, and it must slide in severity in some fashion proportional to the changes in offense seriousness. As adverse publicity is now proposed, it cannot be considered a workable punishment in a system that respects principles of commensurate deserts.

Fines Far and away, cash fines are the most widely imposed sanction against corporations for criminal misconduct.[26] As demonstrated earlier, however, the amount of the fine designated in present statutory provisions varies independently of the seriousness of the offense, at least if one views seriousness as harm risked or caused, plus culpability. This is true of the actual imposition of fines as well. The disparity between amount and offense seriousness is due to a wide variety of circumstances, not the least of which is the desire to bring about some general or specific deterrent impact.[27] Yet, can fines be structured in a way that satisfies desert requirements?

Just Deserts for Corporate Criminals

Recall once again that desert provides only limiting guides for determining the cardinal magnitude of the fine scale for corporations. It is difficult to claim that the most serious kind of corporate crime *deserves* a fine of $200 million, $500 million, or some other astronomical figure. One alternative to this problem is to rely on the amount of the harm, expressed in dollars, caused by the various groups of offenses. Thus, the maximum fine imposed (or the upper bounds of the punishment scale) would be derived according to knowledge of the average injury caused in dollar amounts in the typical case of the most serious corporate crime. Calculating the financial loss caused by a corporate offense is, after all, one way by which harm is defined by many courts and legal commentators. And considerable effort is made in a similar fashion when it comes to determining compensation for damages in tort law for offenses causing harm to economic interests and, increasingly, for offenses that harm other less easily quantifiable interests, such as physical or mental health.[28] Since desert provides no specific answers, why not incorporate a similar procedure into the determination of the criminal fine?

It seems that having a general understanding of the actual physical harms caused by certain kinds of offenses would be helpful in assessing the general seriousness of crime by providing information on how specific interests are affected. Yet, desert in no way entails that the amount of the fine approximates the monetary damage caused or risked by the offense. By scaling fines in such a manner, the condemnatory aspect of punishment and the entire notion of desert would become greatly distorted. First, the entire punishment structure would no longer be tied closely to the expression of condemnation that the fines are said to represent; the focus of punishment, instead, would shift to compensation for damages. Second, it would be impossible to maintain any degree of ordi-

nal proportionality. If the emphasis turned toward the monetary loss caused by certain offenses, parity would undoubtedly
be threatened. In addition, certain economic offenses might
well result in greater dollar loss than offenses that harm interests to life or the environment and that are likely to be considered more total than economic harm. Punishing such crimes
more severely than offenses causing death (on the basis of the
dollar loss) would violate proportionality in rank order and render the reprobative function of the punishments meaningless.
As Joel Feinberg observes:

> What justice demands is that the *condemnatory aspect* of the pun-
> ishment suit the crime, that the crime be of a kind that is truly
> worthy of reprobation. Further, the degree of disapproval ex-
> pressed by the punishment should "fit" the crime only in the un-
> problematic sense that the more serious crimes should receive
> stronger disapproval than the less serious ones, the seriousness of
> the crime being determined by the amount of the harm it generally
> causes and the degree to which people are disposed to commit
> it. . . . Given our conventions, of course, condemnation is ex-
> pressed by hard treatment, and the degree of harshness of the latter
> expresses the degree of reprobation of the former. *Still, this should
> not blind us to the fact that it is social disapproval and its approxi-
> mate expression that should fit the crime and not hard treatment as
> such.* (emphasis added)[29]

Desert does not require that the sum of the fines somehow
comport to the economic costs of the offense either cardinally
or ordinally. What is required is that crimes that rate high on a
scale of offense seriousness receive fines that are rated as severe on a punishment scale, and that the fines for other offenses
are graded accordingly.

Constructing a punishment scale based on fines creates additional problems. One is the issue of overspill, mentioned
briefly in chapter 2. As John Coffee sees it:

> Axiomatically, corporations do not bear the ultimate cost of the fine;
> put simply, when the corporation catches a cold, someone else
> sneezes. This overspill of the penalty initially imposed on the cor-

poration has at least four distinct levels, each progressively more serious. First, stockholders bear the penalty in the reduced value of their securities. Second, bondholders and other creditors suffer a diminution in the value of their securities which reflects the increased riskiness of the enterprise. . . . [T]he third level incidence of a severe financial penalty involves parties even less culpable than the stockholders. . . . [I]f the fine is severe enough to threaten the solvency of the corporation, the predictable response will be a cost-cutting campaign, involving reductions in the work force through layoffs of lower echelon employees who receive no benefits from the earlier crime. . . . Finally, there is the fourth level of incidence of a financial penalty: it may be passed on to the consumer. If the corporation competes in a product market characterized by imperfect competition . . . then the fine may be recovered from the consumer in the form of higher prices. If this happens, the "wicked" corporation not only goes unpunished, but the intended beneficiary of the criminal statute (i.e., the consumer) winds up bearing its penalty.[30]

Several observations are in order regarding the problem of overspill. First, it is clear that the external impact of corporate fines runs counter to desert principles. Only those deemed blameworthy for an offense merit punishment. Yet, while such impact may occur in theory, there is little empirical evidence to demonstrate exactly how those fines are distributed and the extent (and consequence) to which those who are supposed to absorb the cost actually do. This is not to discount the significance of the criticism, only to say that the impact of fines is a subject that merits much greater academic attention, since it affects the way in which corporations are punished, regardless of the philosophical foundation of the punishment.

Second, as a number of commentators have pointed out, at least some of those exposed to an overspill effect may have less ground to claim injustice than at first thought. An argument can be made that the further one is removed from any benefits that may accrue from an action, the less culpable one is for it. Certainly stockholders and bondholders stand to benefit from certain kinds of undetected improper behavior. It makes sense, then, that where they stand to benefit, they ought as well stand to suffer consequences if the corporation's illegal activity is detected.[31] No doubt, the greater the loss that is imposed on such individuals, the more concern will, and should, be generated.

However, many mechanisms are available to protect groups from such consequences. First, nothing inherently binds them to their securities in the corporation. There is a lag time between investigation, indictment, conviction, and punishment that affords ample opportunities for stockholders and bondholders to divest their interests in the firm and to remove themselves from the possible impact of punishment. Moreover, stockholders have the option of recovering damages against the corporation through civil suits that may arise from the criminal activity.[32]

The impact of the external costs of fines on consumers is more problematic. Once again, caution is necessary because of the lack of information about this impact. While corporations may pass on the cost of the fine to consumers, the likelihood of their doing so probably depends on the nature of the market in which they operate and their standing within it. There are certain to be price constraints operating naturally on many corporations that prohibit them from raising prices. Passing on the cost of punishment to consumers, then, is probably not an immediate response, but the result of complex calculations on the feasibility and impact of doing so. The point here is that overspill to consumers is not necessarily "automatic," as has been recently claimed. Much more information is needed on these calculations before such claims can be made with the authority with which they have been spouted to date.

Perhaps more important, the establishment of a set dollar figure for any given offense is certainly bound to create disproportionate burdens on different corporate offenders convicted of that crime. Corporations, like individuals, vary greatly in wealth. When it is unevenly distributed, those corporations that do not possess the necessary resources will be punished inordinately in comparison to more wealthy offenders.

Day Fines   One possible way to overcome this lack of parity is to adopt, at the corporate level, a system similar to the day-fine method now used in Scandinavia, Great Britain, Cuba, and Mexico.[33] The concept is not new. Evidence of the principle underlying day fines can be traced to thirteenth-century England, where amercements were fixed by the offender's neighbors according to wealth.[34] At the Sixth International Penal and Penitentiary Congress in 1900, the procurator of France noted that "when a laborer is fined the equivalent of three days' wages, equity and efficiency of sentence require that a wealthy man be fined three days' income for the same offense."[35]

The day fine for individuals has two components. First, it is expressed in discrete units, whose number varies between the minimum and maximum amounts prescribed for the offense. (The number of units therefore represents the measure of punishment.) In Sweden, for example, the number of units for day fines is no less than 1 and no more than 120. Second, the monetary value of the unit is determined on the basis of the wealth of the offender, his daily income, his productive capacity, and the number of his dependents. Thus, distinctions in punishment are made according to the individual's economic status so as to ensure equity in severity. In Sweden, the per diem amount of a day fine varies from 10 to 1,000 kronor (one kronor equals about fifteen cents). Given these figures, the highest punishment that may be imposed in one sentence for one offense is 120,000 kronor (120 units times 1,000 kronor).[36]

The first step in developing a workable day-fine system is to determine the means by which the monetary value of the day-fine units may be calculated. Here the task is to define the relevant criteria as expressions of corporate wealth, and to delimit additional factors necessary in determining an offender's ability to pay.

Day fines for individuals generally entail two components, the offender's income and the offender's existing wealth. Two individuals with similar incomes but differing assets will be disproportionately burdened by similar fines. The same holds true for corporations. Given size and financial complexity, there are obviously more substantial problems when the offender is a corporation. Nonetheless, all corporations must by law undergo a financial audit conducted by an accredited accounting firm. These examinations must also comply with relatively rigid guidelines that reflect consistency in the means by which financial status is determined across corporations.

As a result of the annual audit, all corporations will have data pertaining to yearly income. This information is normally passed on to shareholders through annual reports. These statements of income reflect revenues generated from products or services, income from other sources, and expenses incurred during the year (for example, wages, salaries and payroll expenses, other operating expenses, and interest expenses). Net income will reflect revenues, less expenses and provisions for income taxes.

Furthermore, the annual review will supply information about the corporation's assets and liabilities, the indicators of its wealth. Balance sheets will record the corporation's current assets, including its cash on hand, accounts receivable, inventories, prepaid insurance, and such other miscellaneous assets as equity in undistributed earnings, notes receivable, and certificates of deposit. Included here as assets are the corporation's property (plant and equipment less accumulated depreciation and amortization). Balance sheets reflecting the corporation's liabilities will include such items as notes payable to banks, accounts payable, accrued salaries and wages, and accrued taxes. Liabilities will also reflect reserves for losses, long-term notes payable, deferred income taxes, and shareholders' interest.

Constructing the punishment-severity scale must incorporate both income and wealth. Fines targeted at income alone would be more easily absorbed by corporations with vast assets. Similarly, annual corporate-income levels tend to vary greatly from year to year, making income an unreliable indicator of corporate financial status. At the same time, assets alone do not easily reflect important changes that may occur during the course of a year—developments that are important relative to the corporation's ability to pay. Failure to calculate income in instances where a corporation operated at a loss over the year may result in an unwanted overspill effect. Similarly, vast profits made by a firm over a recent period (perhaps even the product of the criminal activity in question) may not be discovered by examining corporate wealth alone.

A corporate day-fine system would base the amount of the fine on a percentage of income and a percentage of wealth. As crimes grow more severe, the amount of the fine would increase incrementally as a greater percentage of both income and wealth. A punishment system designed in this fashion would maintain proportionality in the relative severity of corporate offenses, thus protecting the principle of rank order. At the same time, the punishment system considers the differences in corporations' ability to pay, which protects concerns for parity.

Of central importance is the manner in which the cardinal magnitude of the punishment scale would be determined. The cardinal magnitude reflects the maximum and minimum levels of the fine that anchor the punishment scale: should the fine be 100 percent of the corporation's annual income or 10 percent? As noted earlier, desert provides few guides on this point. To the extent that it helps set outer limits, one possible way to establish cardinal magnitude would be to determine, in an *a priori* fashion, the most and least amounts of punishment one is willing to impose (given the impact that fines have in general on corporations) and then fix the ordinal ranking of the scale accordingly. Perhaps fining a corporation 100 percent of its annual income constitutes a virtual death penalty and may therefore be overly severe.

It may be possible to calculate the cardinal magnitude by other rationales, such as deterrence. A scale with the most severe fine representing 5 percent of a corporations's annual income may well be regarded as having no impact as a negative profit contingency to be considered in rationally determining conduct (assuming, of course, that corporations do consider such things). To the extent that desert parameters provide room for expansion, deterrence may serve as the rationale for the increase. However, once the outer limits are fixed, ordinal-proportionality requirements serve as the guides for setting the rest of the grid.

The day-fine system suggested here confronts the problems related to the disproportional burden that cash fines impose on different corporations that vary in wealth. Cash fines and equity fines both suffer from the spillover effects of punishments. To what extent does the day fine eliminate this dilemma? Clearly, not entirely. The fines may yet result in negative repercussions for consumers, employers, suppliers, and others. However, the day-fine system provides a means for addressing such concerns. It may be possible, for example, to discover on a case-by-case basis when the fine is likely to spill over to others. It is entirely possible to determine the point at which an incremental increase in punishment would require the corporation to take steps to consolidate its units or to streamline its ventures, resulting in layoffs or similar ramifications. Such findings can then be weighed in deciding whether to impose the fine designated by the grid or to deviate from the grid and reduce the fine to a level not threatening to corporate survival.

What impact would the day-fine system have on corporate punishment? First and foremost, such a structure would provide a systematic strategy for imposing fines against corporations that focuses on maintaining parity and ordinal proportionality. Yet, important concerns remain open to investigation.

Whether such a system of fines does in fact maximize equality merits further consideration. It is possible that a corporation that has been a leader in the market, possesses large assets, and is diversified into a variety of activities may be much more capable of weathering the impact of a fine than a smaller, less competitive corporation, in spite of the fact that the impact of the fine is expressed on paper as being approximately equal. (One could argue that there is a similarity here with the cases of different individuals who, because of upbringing, proximity of family and friends, or worldview, are more capable of weathering a period of incarceration than others serving the same amount of time.) The more knowledge that is gained about the impact of such fines on different offenders, the more likely it is that these problems can be reduced, although it is highly improbable that this unwanted consequence of punishment can ever be remedied entirely.

Furthermore, difficulty may be encountered in determining the offender's ability to pay.[37] Corporations may go to great lengths to hide assets and holdings and to exaggerate liabilities, and computing daily income or convertible property is certain to be difficult.[38] In addition, the amount decided upon will differ significantly, depending on whether the calculation follows the "net method" (based on income after tax deductions) or the "gross method."[39] Yet, continued research in this area is likely to provide some meaningful solutions to these issues.

Suspension of Business Activities   Recalling Baron Thurlow's complaint that corporations have "no souls to damn nor bodies to kick," corporate-punishment theorists often complain that corporations can suffer no punishment comparable to imprisonment. The closest one comes to such a sanction is corporate dissolution. Yet this approach is more akin to capital punishment than to imprisonment, with the added fear that the dead may once again arise, albeit in a somewhat different form.

However, there is one punishment that roughly approximates imprisonment and has been used in a limited form against corporations in a civil context—suspension of business activity.[40] Two types of suspension stand out: suspension of *all* corporate activity for a given period and suspension of *certain* activities for a period. Either form does in essence what imprisonment does to individuals: it takes away their freedom to engage in normal activity—in this case normal business activity—for a set amount of time. An example of such a sanction involves the recent suspension of gambling activity of a major casino in Atlantic City after evidence was found that the casino catered to organized-crime figures.[41] It is also rather common for the regulatory bodies of the various stock and commodities exchanges to suspend certain firms and individuals from trading for weeks or months.[42] One advantage of this form of punishment is that it can be more easily tailored to fit the culpable components in the corporation. Where evidence exists (from looking at the corporation's CID structure) that a large portion of criminal activity stretched throughout the corporation, then total suspension might be appropriate. Where evidence indicates criminal activity in particular markets or units of the cor-

171

poration, then suspension of only those market activities appears more justifiable.

However, from a desert perspective there remain substantial problems with corporate suspension. First, it may be very difficult to equate the time and type of suspension with the actual impact of the punishment. While one can arbitrarily quantify the time as, for example, six months, there is little understanding of the harshness of that suspension. One could make a counterargument that such a dilemma is no more problematic than it is in the case of imprisonment of individuals. What *is* the impact or consequence of imprisoning someone for five years? What does it do in a general sense to an inmate's perception of reality, his relationship with significant others, his likelihood of future earnings? In particular, how does a sentence of five years differ from a sentence of two years in these respects? On the other hand, calculations may be easier with corporations because of the priority they place on financial security. It may be true that corporations value reputation as a quality independent of earnings, and that they maintain jobs for individuals and provide services for the consumer, but corporations do not exist to have a reputation, nor to provide services, nor to supply people with jobs. It may therefore be possible to come to a better understanding of the impact arising from the suspension of operations for a given period.

The question remains, How would requirements of ordinal proportionality be satisfied with this form of punishment—in particular the requirement of parity? Ultimately, such suspensions may well have dramatically different consequences for different corporations, even though both were suspended for the same period. Although this problem appears to be difficult to resolve, it may be possible to adopt a suspension system similar to the day-fine system suggested earlier. Under such a plan, each corporation would receive the same number of units of suspension, but the amount of the unit for each corporation would be calculated on the basis of the corporation's individual ability to withstand such a suspension.

At this point there is insufficient information on the impact of suspension of corporate activities for this strategy to be adopted in a corporate sentencing system. Yet, such a sanction may become a feasible alternative to the fine and come to more closely resemble imprisonment for individuals. Much more research needs to be done on this type of penalty, perhaps beginning with an evaluation of the impact of similar sanctions that have been imposed already in the civil context.

SANCTIONS FOR INDIVIDUAL AGENTS

Constructing a punishment scale for persons involved in corporate offenses does not differ in significant ways from developing such a scale for offenders who commit common crimes. The most severe punishment that may be imposed against white-collar offenders is imprisonment, and, following the claims of desert theorists, its use should be reserved for serious corporate offenses. The scale of offense seriousness, determined by the harm of the crime and the culpability of the agent, should serve as the guide by which punishment severity is graded. Controlling for aggravating and mitigating circumstances, parity is ensured by punishing offenses that are equal in seriousness similarly, and rank order is ensured by grading the relative severity of punishments in a manner that reflects the relative seriousness of the offense.

Crime-Control Considerations and
Cardinal Proportionality

Finally, because desert offers no exact guides in determining either the maximum or minimum levels of punishment (or, where imprisonment is used, guides to determine whether to use it instead of other forms of punishment) such other factors as penal resources, categorical incapacitation, or deterrence may be useful aids in making these decisions.[43]

Penal resources, particularly prison capacity, have been considered in determining where to begin the use of imprisonment on the scale of offense severity. Consideration of prison-space availability seems ironic here, given the low rate of imprisonment of corporate offenders. Yet, such a factor could be adopted when and if prison capacity becomes a concern in federal sentencing.[44]

Von Hirsch has attempted a cautious synthesis of crime-prevention aims and desert considerations, focusing specifically on the use of categorical incapacitation. Yet, concerns for categorical incapacitation seem insignificant with respect to individuals involved in corporate crimes. Although extensive data do not exist, it is unlikely that corporate agents as a group, or agents involved in specific types of activities, represent a picture of career-criminal conduct with high rates of serious recidivism that has been portrayed for some varieties of common crime.[45]

Yet, von Hirsch does mention that general deterrence may also come into play in making cardinal-proportionality determinations:

> Consider a system which used imprisonment as the penalty only for serious offenses, and suppose the question is whether the scale should run up to the maximum prison terms of five years or ten. Either maximum would be consistent with the limit of commensurateness . . . : the penalties would be severe, but this would be permissible since the offenses are serious. It therefore becomes appropriate to consider how much more deterrent effect, overall, an up-to-ten-year scale is likely to have than an up-to-five year scale. Unless the ten-year scale was expected to have substantially greater deterrent effect, the lower magnitude would be preferred.[46]

Scaling Punishments

In principle, then, such inclusion of general-deterrence concerns would be permissible in determining where the imprisonment line is to be drawn with respect to individual offenders, as well as to the overall magnitude of the punishment scale. Furthermore, while penalties applicable to corporations as entities are limited, such deterrence concerns may be applied in principle to the determination of the magnitude of the fine scale. It is crucial to stress that although deterrence may be considered in establishing the overall amount of punishment to be imposed, it may not be applied to specific kinds of corporate crimes, such as insider trading, because of the desire to call attention to and to prevent that particular violation. Such a practice is commonly called for in both corporate sentencing theory and practice. Yet, this policy violates concerns for ordinal proportionality; mainly, it creates more severe punishments for one offense category than for another on the basis of something other than the comparative seriousness of the crimes.

Caution must be exercised, however, in applying these deterrence concerns. Earlier, I claimed that although deterrence suffices for many as the principal justification for allocating corporate criminal punishments, empirical evidence is lacking to demonstrate any enhanced deterrent effects generated through increased punishment. This lack of empirical data does not mean, however, that a deterrent effect may not exist with this type of criminal activity; more research is certainly needed in this respect. What must be emphasized is that the focus of such a punishment system should be on desert as opposed to deterrence. To concentrate on maximizing deterrence benefits within ordinal desert constraints may create the risk of losing sight of the intentions of a desert-based punishment system.

CHAPTER 9

The Application and
Limits of Desert

THIS STUDY has addressed the role of desert in the punishment of corporations and their agents. My approach has been twofold. First, I have examined the general rationale for desert as a basis for criminal punishment. The focus here has been on why corporate legal theorists writing on punishment have rejected desert in this role. Second, this study has reviewed the general principles of desert and the allocation of punishment and has addressed the specific issues that confront the application of these principles in the context of corporate crime.

There is a growing concern about the harms committed by corporate illegality, a concern not limited to academia but shared by the general public as well. One product of this attitude is increased attention to the means by which we control and punish corporate crime. Traditional utilitarian crime-control strategies (deterrence, incapacitation, and rehabilitation) are proffered but are often found wanting. Sentencing systems based on desert, on the other hand, have been limited in scope, focusing largely on the more traditional crimes of individuals. Those writing on desert have not addressed, in any systematic fashion, how principles of commensurate deserts apply to the complex crimes of large organizations and their agents. This concluding chapter summarizes the major components of desert-based sentencing systems as they apply to corporate crime and suggests some directions for future research.

THE COMPONENTS OF A DESERT-BASED PUNISHMENT SYSTEM

Unlike a utilitarian-based corporate-punishment system, which looks to the reduction of crime as the central rationale for the distribution of punishments, a sentencing system founded on desert focuses on the condemnatory implications of punishment as the basis for allocating sentences. Although utilitarian principles may serve as the central justification for the existence of punishment, it also reflects reprobation for wrongful conduct.[1] This reprobative function serves not only as an added feature to ensure crime prevention, but also has an independent role valued by society.

Given that the distinguishing feature of criminal punishment lies in its condemnatory function, the distribution of punishments—involving both the questions of liability (who should be punished?) and amount (how much?)—is to be based on past behavior and not on the likelihood of future misconduct. A desert-based corporate-punishment system imposes penalties for corporations as entities and for the individuals acting on behalf of corporations, where the evidence demonstrates that the company or the individual, respectively, is to blame for the offense.

At least in legal theory, the question of liability for persons in the corporate setting has not been particularly troublesome. Individuals are to be held accountable when evidence demonstrates that they were aware of the activity and that the act could not have occurred without their participation. This holds true for managers and directors who command or authorize the act, either implicitly or explicitly, and for lower-level employees who directly engage in the act, regardless of their distance from the decision-making centers in the corporation. In spite of the law's apparent clarity, much more work remains to be done in this area. Human interaction in organizational settings has received much attention in the field of administrative behavior and the sociology of work, but it has appeared only recently in the literature of the law. The question of individual responsibility for actions that take place within groups merits much more attention in the future.

The focus of this book, however, is on the corporation, where the question of corporate liability poses troublesome concerns for a law based on the actions of individuals. Some commentators have expressed reservations about the imposition of liability on corporations on the grounds that firms cannot act with any real intent. For the most part, corporate liability is viewed principally as a legal fiction by which corporate-crime control is maximized.[2]

Yet, it has been suggested here that corporations *as* corporations can be held accountable for their actions by virtue of the very reasons that underlie incorporation. Corporations are formed to engage in and facilitate activity impossible for individuals acting as a group of singular persons. Such firms may be held accountable, therefore, when the wrongful conduct reflects corporate policy in some fashion or other. The wrongful conduct did not depend, in other words, on any specific individual or individuals, but on the arrangements or patterns that make up the organization.[3] Those configurations can be demonstrated by examining, specifically, the "corporate internal decision structure," consisting of the firm's flowchart, policies, and procedural rules.[4]

From a desert perspective, the amount of punishment is to be based on the seriousness of the criminal conduct. As a first step, then, corporate offenses must be assessed and ranked by seriousness, a concept that entails both the harm of the act and the culpability of the actor. Each of these components includes a set of procedures or guides that may be considered.

Although corporate-offense seriousness may be ranked by popular surveys of perceived offense severity, such polls are unlikely to provide the information that is desired from a desert perspective. Popular surveys do not generally consider enough information on the different types of injury produced by offenses, nor do they consider such factors as culpability, excuses, and circumstances that are important in the assessment of seriousness. Most important the concept of harm entails injury to certain interests, and surveys at present do not provide systematic rankings of interests in any meaningful way.[5]

The process of assessing and ranking corporate-offense seriousness must begin with a systematic evaluation and ordering of the interests that are harmed by the criminal offenses. The concept of interests is complex, entailing myriad values and goals that exist within the context of different cultures and different times.[6] While it is clear that judges do consider these interests in their sentencing decisions, it is equally clear (as pointed out by Stanton Wheeler, Kenneth Mann, and Austin Sarat) that there is little consensus about what these interests mean exactly and, more problematically, the weight they should be given.[7] The model that has been suggested here—delineating those generic interests, such as physical well-being, safety, and property, which, when harmed, merit punishment—serves as one starting point to begin to overcome this dissensus. Using the concept of inclusivity, or the degree to which harm to one interest results in harm to other interests, the concerns may be ranked by relative priority. They could then be scaled further to reflect the relative level of the interest—welfare, security, or accumulative—meriting the greatest priority.[8] While this model is not suggested as a panacea for the problems, such guidelines serve as a starting point to build a common understanding—or to use Wheeler, Mann, and Sarat's term, "a jurisprudence of harm."

These interests pertain largely to individual victimization. A large variety of corporate misconduct affects a broader level of public interests. And, while all corporate offenses are violations of trust, it is the offenses against public interests that are most typically associated with trust. It is possible to scale crimes affecting public interest in a fashion similar to that outlined for individual concerns.

Having established the scale of interests, the next step entails examining the different types of corporate offenses and classifying each in relation to the scale. This process may be conducted by consulting the various statutes describing the offenses or by referring to other information, such as victimization studies, that depicts the injury typical of the offense.

Once corporate crimes are ranked according to harm, the next step involves the assessment of culpability factors that enter into such an assessment. Given the deterrent focus of the existing theory of corporate liability, it is not useful to rely on existing concepts of liability to provide the standards of fault to be incorporated for the purposes of sentencing; separate criteria are needed.[9]

One method would be to scale culpability according to the Model Penal Code standards, which consider whether the actor engaged in the activity purposefully, knowingly, recklessly, or negligently.[10] When the offender is an individual, factors related to command, authorization, acquiescence, and reckless supervision could be taken into consideration.[11]

The level of culpability assigned to the corporation would not be based on the actions of its officers and employees, but would be determined by examining the corporation's flow-chart, procedural rules, and company policies. Thus, controlling for harm, when the corporate internal decision structure indicates that the actions were of a corporate nature, and when that information suggests the acts were carried out purposefully, the corporation would merit the most serious punishment.

Having initially scaled the conduct according to these distinctions, the next step would be to consider any aggravating and mitigating conditions that might be relevant to the assessment of culpability. In the instance where the corporation is involved, factors relating to the firm's prior record and to its reactive policy may be considered. When the individual is involved, such aggravating and mitigating factors would include duress, degree of actor's involvement, and ignorance of the law. [12]

Given that corporate-offense seriousness may be assessed and ranked, what considerations enter into the construction of the sentencing scale? Two concerns guide its development. The first involves ordinal proportionality. Desert serves as the guide here, as the severity of the punishment, in terms of parity and rank order of offenses, must be scaled in proportion to the gravity of the offense. [13]

The second concern in the construction of a desert-based sentencing system involves the cardinal magnitude of the punishment scale. The concept of proportionality lends guidance here, but it does not, by itself, indicate specific solutions to questions about the absolute severity of a punishment scale or the location (anchoring points) at which certain kinds of punishments are appropriate. To the extent that desert affords only limiting guides for determining the cardinal magnitude of the punishment scale, it is possible that other rationales, such as concern for general deterrence, enter into the consideration, granted that such rationales do not violate the outer limits established by desert concerns or create disproportionate punishments with regard to the ordinal levels of punishment.[14]

On the basis of these requirements, certain punishments now in use or suggested as alternatives—such as structural intervention or adverse publicity (as each is now structured for corporations)—are not appropriate in a desert-based punishment structure.[15] Fines are feasible punishment, given certain cautions. In particular, fines must be structured to result in proportional burdens for different offenders and to reduce the likelihood of overspill to consumers or employees. To minimize these problems, a day-fine system—where the severity of the fine is represented in fixed units, but the amount of the units assessed depends on the corporation's ability to pay—may be implemented.[16] In the case of individuals meriting severe punishments, imprisonment serves as the sanction most likely to be used for serious offenses, with nonprison alternatives available for lesser offenses. A day-fine system could also be incorporated in such cases.

Some Limitations of Desert

As with a system based on utilitarian considerations, a corporate-punishment system based on principles of desert raises a number of important problems and concerns. Certainly one issue that permeates all punishment systems, but perhaps stands out in a system grounded so firmly in the blaming features of punishment, involves the question of whose interests will be considered in the scaling of offense seriousness. The guides outlined earlier provide some systematic standards by which those interests can be evaluated and ranked. Nonetheless, the interests that are ultimately scaled are likely to reflect the preferences of those who scale them, and these preferences may vary widely depending on whether the scaler is "conservative," "liberal," "libertarian," "humanist," or is swayed by any other political ideology. Central to the concept of desert is the reprobative value of punishment for morally wrongful conduct. Punishments announce to the offender, on behalf of society, its moral sentiments. The interests delineated by a sentencing commission and ultimately ranked in order of importance are thus announcements of the morality valued by society to be fostered and protected by the criminal law. The degree to which the selection and scaling of interests actually represents the interests of society, as opposed to the interests of those who are chosen to sit in judgment, is open to debate.[17]

Other issues concerning the scaling of offense seriousness merit attention as well. It was suggested in chapter 7 that the harms caused by corporate offenses be defined by the damage rendered in the *typical* case. Yet, these offenses are often characterized by a large range of damage. Pollution offenses are perhaps the best example here. Such violations may range from small spills causing little damage to very large spills, such as that in Alaska when the *Exxon Valdez* ran aground, that kill millions of fish and plants, destroy recreational areas, ruin aquatic industries, and cost millions or billions of dollars to clean up. It would be unjust to punish both offenses similarly. One way to overcome this problem is to rank the harms by the degree of damage done; in other words, according to whether the damage affected welfare, security, or accumulative interests. Yet, even with this further distinction, it is possible that the range within any one of those levels is again so large as to render punishment for that typical offense unfair.[18]

A more important concern involves the method by which particular offenses will be classified with regard to the harm they do. The procedure suggested here is to consult the statutory descriptions of the offense for details of the kinds of harm inflicted. Yet, the problems encountered in this approach are the same as those encountered with popular perceptions of offense seriousness. Harm is not what one perceives it to be, but what in fact it *is*.[19] Statutory descriptions may be a poor means by which to delineate details about the types of injury done to specific interests, particularly in terms of whether or not certain activities affect the more specific levels of harms (welfare, security, accumulative) that have to be incorporated in the scale of offense severity. One solution is to turn to empirical studies of the harm that actually takes place with certain kinds of offenses—either case studies, or more beneficially, corporate-crime victimization studies. Unfortunately, neither of these is easy to come by. Given this present limitation of data, the most feasible approach is to rank offenses in terms of their harm by consulting statutory descriptions of the offense and, as more information becomes available, adjust those rankings accordingly.

Determining where the harm to community or public interests stands in relation to harms to other interests merits further attention. At this point, a workable, but less systematic, solution to this dilemma is to rank offenses to community interests in relation to other offenses and to then attempt to reach some consensus on where those harms lie on the scale. Again, much more theoretical work is needed on the independent value of community interests and on the importance of such interests in relation to their role in maximizing the attainment and fulfillment of other individual interests.

It was noted earlier that efforts to increase the deterrent impact of corporate punishments have been hampered by the difficulty of locating criminal responsibility in the corporate setting. Assessing culpability of both the corporation and the individuals involved for the purposes of scaling offense seriousness will involve similar dilemmas. Determining the degree of individual fault (purpose, knowledge, negligence, or recklessness—in descending order of seriousness) will be difficult, given the "institutionalization of irresponsibility" created by the structure, size, and reliance on delegation of duties characterizing large organizations.[20]

Determining corporate responsibility is certain to be difficult as well. Guides that focus on the corporation's internal decision structure will be hampered by the extensive and often contradictory evidence brought to bear to describe the corporation's flowchart, policies, and procedural rules. Further complications are certain to arise given the limited resources, manpower, and time available to agencies charged with the responsibility of determining fault.[21] The result is likely to be a reduction in the number of cases in which higher degrees of fault (purpose and knowledge) are established, as well as an increase in cases involving negligence or recklessness.[22] The importance of cases of negligence or recklessness notwithstanding, this is certain to cause some clamor among those who want to see a tougher stance taken against corporations, regardless of the implications that goal has for concepts of desert.

Offense seriousness entails the combination of harm and culpability, yet little has been written on how the two concepts work together to comprise this important component. Should it first be scaled in terms of harm, and then modified according to the degree of fault, or vice versa? Because of the difficulty in coming to agreement about the harm caused by a given offense, John Kleinig has suggested that greater emphasis be placed on the concept of fault in determining the proper punishment.[23] He provides little assistance, however, when it comes to indicating just how this might be accomplished. At this point, the most workable solution is to hold culpability constant and scale the harm itself. Having scaled the offenses on that basis, lesser degrees of fault may be considered in reducing the seriousness of the offense. Much more work needs to be done in this area to provide better guidance on how these two components of seriousness interact.

Finally, some issues remain in locating the anchoring points of a punishment scale. Because principles of desert are vague in this area, such other factors as penal resources and general deterrence may be considered in establishing the anchors. No accurate data exist, however, on the deterrent impact that may result from adjusting the anchoring point upwards or downwards. The inclusion of other criteria may turn attention away from the major tenet of a desert-based system—that the punishments reflect the seriousness of the offenses, and not crime-control considerations per se.

Regardless of other criteria that may be used, the concept of desert is vital in establishing the anchoring points of the scale. To this extent, it is likely that some agreement can be reached about the most serious and least serious punishments that may be imposed.[24] These decisions rest, however, on what is known or believed about the consequences and impact of these respective punishments on the offender being punished; and those who have written on desert have not, in any systematic fashion, considered these important issues. Much can be learned through empirical research to help in this regard. Just as victimization surveys and case studies assist in determining the actual harms of certain kinds of corporate crimes, studies of the impact and consequences of various punishments imposed on corporations (fines, suspensions, adverse publicity) and individuals (fines, incarceration, suspension from practice) will shed light on the harshness of the sanctions and provide a clearer rationale for determining the amount to be imposed.

Just Deserts for Corporate Criminals

Granted, it is unlikely that total consensus will be reached on the propriety of these punishments, but the more information available, the more solid the grounds for making various claims of propriety.

CONCLUSION

This book has examined the specific issues that arise in developing a punishment system based on the principles of commensurate deserts. Many of the concepts important to desert are normative concerns ("harm," "culpability," and "deserved punishment," for example) and are thus susceptible to different interpretations. But that different people interpret them differently is not grounds for their dismissal. Indeed, that they are widely accepted as important principles in sentencing among judges and policymakers alike is testament to the need to develop a jurisprudence of desert for corporate crime that provides a starting point for a common frame of reference. Furthermore, popular misconceptions to the contrary notwithstanding, the principles upon which desert is based are not intended as precise, mechanical terms to be calculated with the certainty that one calculates a sum. They are guides, with certain rules to be sure, but guides nonetheless. To this extent they are concepts that may be organized and systematized in a fashion characterized by rationality and consideration. And it is through this process that the central concerns of desert advocates—fairness and proportionality—are addressed.

Continued empirical research on many of these areas (the extent of harm, the determination of culpability in a corporate setting, individual behavior in corporations, and the effects of fines and imprisonment on offenders, to name a few) will go a long way in providing information on which these rational determinations can be made.

Application and Limits of Desert

While much work is left to be done, it is possible to make considered and systematic choices in the design of a desert-based punishment system for corporate offenses. The harms of such crimes may be scaled on the basis of the interests affected, and the degree to which those interests have been damaged. Corporate and individual culpability can be assessed and ranked in a systematic manner, taking into consideration the specific concerns that have been raised by organizational theorists about corporate behavior and about responsibility in the corporate setting. The anchoring points and magnitudes of the corporate punishment scale can be established, and offenses and the punishment imposed for them may be aligned in a manner that satisfies the requirements of ordinal proportionality.

Taking steps in this direction would surely be an improvement over current corporate-sentencing practices. While judges may have a general sense of the aims they hope to achieve through sentencing, the fact remains that contemporary corporate-sentencing policy is asystematic and piecemeal. Much of this may be a result of judges' efforts to satisfy all the intended goals that are typically associated with punishment, deterrence, desert, and, to a certain extent, rehabilitation. Yet, efforts to address all goals in the individual sentences handed down are not only doomed to failure in the instant cases, since many of these goals are incompatible, but they also produce wide disparities in sentencing practices among different offenders and for similar kinds of offenses over time. Sentencing policy without systematic guides applied by all is not a "policy" in any normal meaning of the term.

A final word is needed here on the relationship between theory and practice. Wheeler, Mann, and Sarat rightly note the importance of establishing a "closer dialogue between those who do justice and those who write about it."[25] Those who write about moral and legal philosophy come from a tradition vastly different from that of the scholar steeped in empirical research and worlds apart from that of the practitioner. It is often difficult to know how the three can possibly interact in any meaningful way. Usually they do not. Much of what the legal philosopher constructs comes from a history of ideas rather than from a history of actions. The process is meaningful in the same way that an architect's original blueprints create a rational order among basic structural and mechanical principles. Architecture done well simplifies these principles; it hones and refines, and from it emerges ordered concepts and structures; and architecture is made better for it. That is the purpose of a model. Yet, for all the value that is derived from the original sketch, the ultimate purpose is to erect a building. What appears on blueprints must by necessity change to meet the demands of real-world forces. Thus, the interaction between the architect and those who are most aware of these forces—the contractor, the owner, the occupant—is crucial.

The interaction must begin with the understanding of each individual reference point. The architect cannot merely draw a plan on the basis of what other buildings look like, or on the whims of the contractor or occupant. To do so is to lose sight of the principles upon which architecture rests. The model is vital. At the same time, the architect cannot stand on principle alone, only to suffer the fate of Howard Rourke in Ayn Rand's *Fountainhead*.[26] The model must adapt to those who will use it.

So it goes with persons interested in sentencing policy—or in any other social policy, for that matter. Policymakers and practitioners must recognize and acknowledge the value of a model—a jurisprudence—that brings order to principles. Moral and legal philosophers must recognize that, for a variety of reasons, principles often do not flow in an orderly direction and that compromise and change become necessary.

This being said, here, then, is one model. Further attention, both theoretical and empirical, from academics and practitioners alike is encouraged so as to continue the development and refinement of sentencing practices in the area of corporate crime.

Notes

CHAPTER 1

1. Marshall Clinard et al., *Illegal Corporate Behavior* (Washington, D.C.: U.S. Government Printing Office, 1979), p. 17.

2. For a discussion of the problems of defining white-collar crime, see Ronald Kramer, "Corporate Criminality, the Development of an Idea," in *Corporations as Criminals*, ed. Ellen Hochstedler (Beverly Hills, Calif.: Sage, 1984), pp. 13–37; Herbert Edelhertz, *The Nature, Impact, and Prosecution of White-Collar Crime* (Washington, D.C.: U.S. Government Printing Office, 1970); and Gilbert Geis and Ezra Stotland, *White-Collar Crime: Theory and Research* (Beverly Hills, Calif.: Sage, 1980).

3. Clinard et al., *Illegal Corporate Behavior*, p. 17.

4. Ibid., p. 20.

5. For a critique of the Clinard and Yeager study on these grounds, see Leonard Orland, "Reflections on Corporate Crime: Law in Search of Theory and Scholarship," *American Criminal Law Review* 17 (1980), pp. 506–10.

6. See Christopher Stone, "The Place of Enterprise Liability in the Control of Corporate Conduct," *Yale Law Journal* 90 (1980), pp. 1–77, and Brent Fisse, "Reconstructing Corporate Criminal Law: Deterrence, Retribution, Fault, and Sanctions," *University of Southern California Law Review* 56 (1983), pp. 1141–1246, to name two.

7. Sir William Blackstone, *Commentaries on the Laws of England*, 4 vols. (Oxford: Clarendon Press, 1765–1769), p. 498.

8. James R. Elkins, "Corporations and the Criminal Law: An Uneasy Alliance," *Kentucky Law Journal* 65 (1976), p. 89.

9. 68 Mass. (2 Gray) 339 (1854).

10. 212 U.S.C., at 494–95.

11. The doctrine of *respondeat superior* ("let the master reply") is a particular instance of vicarious responsibility. See Nicolette Parisi, "Theories of Corporate Criminal Liability," in *Corporations as Criminals*, ed. Hochstedler, p. 65n.6.

12. The courts have also ruled that it is unnecessary that any one agent have specific knowledge that a crime was occurring. A collective knowledge of the group of employees is sufficient to establish liability to the corporation.

13. Without such an interpretation a corporation could escape liability simply by issuing directives prohibiting any illegal conduct by its employees.

14. *Harvard Law Review*, "Developments in the Law—Corporate Crime: Regulating Corporate Behavior through Criminal Sanctions," *Harvard Law Review* 92 (1979), p. 1247.

15. Although no statutes carry a strict liability standard, certain regulatory acts, such as the Federal Food, Drug and Cosmetic Act, and the Refuse Act, have been interpreted by the courts as having "congressional intent to contain a strict liability standard." See U.S. v. Dotterweich, 320 U.S. 277 (1943) (Food, Drug and Cosmetic Act) and U.S. v. U.S. Steel Corp., 328 F. Supp. 354, 356 (1970) (Refuse Act). See *Harvard Law Review*, "Developments in the Law," p. 1260n.86.

16. Ibid., p. 1241.

17. Willfulness entails the defendant's acting deliberately with an awareness of the probable consequences of his act. Willfulness differs from knowledge in that the defendant need not know that he was violating the law, rather only that he realize that he was committing an immoral act. See *Harvard Law Review*, "Developments in the Law," p. 1265n.116.

18. Recklessness involves the conscious disregard of a substantial risk, where such risk constitutes "a gross deviation from the standard of care that a law abiding person would exercise in such a situation." Negligence involves a careless disregard of a risk, where such a risk constitutes "a gross deviation from the standard of care that a reasonable person would exercise in such a situation." *Model Penal Code*, section 2.02(2)(d).

19. To a certain extent, however, the courts have watered down the willfulness requirement by interpreting it to mean that the act had only to be deliberately wrongful. The actor need not have known that the act was illegal. Furthermore, there has been a willingness on the part of the courts to infer intent from the conduct itself. See *Harvard Law Review*, "Developments in the Law," p. 1238, 1260.

20. For example, in 18 U.S.C., 2(b) (1976), an indirect actor can be held criminally liable if, "acting with the state of mind required for the commission of the offense, he causes the other person to engage in conduct that would constitute an offense if engaged in personally by the defendant."

21. A number of courts have recognized that a superior can be held liable if he either explicitly or implicitly authorizes an illegal act, or if

he was aware of a crime being committed or about to be committed but fails to act to prevent it. *Harvard Law Review*, "Developments in the Law," pp. 1265–66.

22. See chapter 7 *infra* for more discussion.

23. The most recent and intensive examination of corporate crime has been carried out by Marshall Clinard and Peter Yeager, *Corporate Crime* (New York: Free Press, 1980). Their study is not without criticism, however. See, for example, Orland, "Reflections on Corporate Crime," pp. 506–10. He regards their work as "misperceived empiricism," stating that their incorporation of administrative violations as part of corporate crime misrepresents the real picture of corporate deviance.

24. Clinard and Yeager, *Corporate Crime*, p. 74.

25. *Harvard Law Review*, "Developments in the Law," p. 1229.

26. According to John Coffee, the vast majority of all actions taken against corporations by U.S. attorneys' offices come from agency referrals. Statement made at the Conference on Corporate Regulation, San Antonio, Texas, November 2–4, 1983.

27. Clinard and Yeager identify four kinds of recalls: voluntary, noncompliance, court-ordered, and unilateral orders by the agency. *Corporate Crime*, pp. 84–85.

28. Many fines issued to corporations stem from violations of these orders. As Clinard and Yeager point out, it is often difficult to distinguish between a punitive response and a remedial response with regard to these orders. *Corporate Crime*, p. 86.

29. See *Harvard Law Review*, "Developments in the Law," pp. 1301–2.

30. See Harry Ball and Lawrence Friedman, "The Use of Criminal Sanction in the Enforcement of Economic Legislation: A Sociological View," *Stanford Law Review* 17 (1965), pp. 197–223.

31. As a consequence, a number of commentators have suggested greater reliance on civil sanctions. See *Harvard Law Review*, "Developments in the Law," pp. 1301–11, and Sanford Kadish, "Some Observations on the Use of Criminal Sanctions in the Enforcement of Economic Regulations," *University of Chicago Law Review* 30 (1963), p. 423.

32. The courts have attempted to clarify whether a given sanction is punitive or remedial in nature. The Supreme Court ruled in Kennedy v. Mendoza-Martinez that the following factors were relevant in distinguishing a civil from a criminal sanction: (1) whether the sanction involves an affirmative disability or restraint; (2) whether it has historically been regarded as punishment; (3) whether it involves a finding of *scienter*; (4) whether it promotes the traditional aims of punishment; (5) whether the behavior to which it applies is already a

crime; (6) whether an alternative purpose to which it may rationally be connected is assignable for it; (7) whether it appears excessive in relation to the alternative purpose assigned. This ruling, however, pertained to sanctions normally provided for common crimes and has not been especially helpful with regard to corporations. See *Harvard Law Review,* "Developments in the Law," pp. 1301–5.

33. Ibid., pp. 1307–11. See also Clinard and Yeager, *Corporate Crime,* pp. 91–93.

34. Clinard and Yeager, *Corporate Crime,* p. 93.

35. Sam D. Fine, "The Philosophy of Enforcement," *Food, Drug and Cosmetic Law Journal* 31 (1976), p. 328.

36. For one example, see Susan Shapiro, *Wayward Capitalists: Target of the Securities and Exchange Commission* (New Haven: Yale University Press, 1984).

37. Civil penalties are easier to obtain largely because there are fewer procedural protections and a relaxed burden-of-proof requirement in civil court. For a further discussion, see *Harvard Law Review,* "Developments in the Law," p. 1311. Also see Alexander Kovel, "A Case for Civil Penalties: Air Pollution Control," *Journal of Urban Law* 46 (1969), pp. 153, 159.

38. See, for example, Stephen Yoder, "Comment: Criminal Sanctions for Corporate Illegality," *Journal of Criminal Law and Criminology* 69 (1978), p. 44; *Harvard Law Review,* "Developments in the Law," p. 1237; Gilbert Geis, "Criminal Penalties for Corporate Criminals," *Criminal Law Bulletin* 8 (1972), pp. 377–92.

39. Francis Cullen, William Maakestadt, and Gray Cavender, *Corporate Crime Under Attack: The Ford Pinto Case and Beyond* (Cincinnati: Anderson Press, 1987). See also Brent Fisse and Peter French, eds., *Corrigible Corporations and Unruly Law* (San Antonio: Trinity University Press, 1985).

40. See Stanton Wheeler, Kenneth Mann, and Austin Sarat, *Sitting in Judgement: The Sentencing of White-Collar Criminals* (New Haven: Yale University Press, 1988).

41. For a general discussion of incapacitation and other sentencing rationales, see Hyman Gross and Andrew von Hirsch, eds., *Sentencing* (New York: Oxford University Press, 1981), pp. 187–300. See also Wheeler, Mann, and Sarat, *Sitting in Judgement,* p. 164.

42. Christopher Stone, *Where the Law Ends: The Social Control of Corporate Behavior* (New York: Harper & Row, 1975), pp. 148–49.

43. See Fisse, "Reconstructing Corporate Criminal Law," pp. 1159–66.

44. Andrew von Hirsch, *Doing Justice: The Choice of Punishments* (New York: Hill and Wang, 1976), p. 11.

45. See Yoder, "Comment: Criminal Sanctions" p. 44; see also Wheeler, Mann, and Sarat, *Sitting in Judgement*, p. 165.

46. See *Yale Law Journal*, "Note: Structural Crime and Institutional Rehabilitation: A New Approach to Corporate Sentencing," *Yale Law Journal* 89 (1979), pp. 353–75; and *Yale Law Journal*, "Note: Judicial Intervention and Organizational Theory: Changing Bureaucratic Behavior and Policy," *Yale Law Journal* 89 (1979), pp. 513–37.

47. See, for example, Fisse, "Reconstructing Corporate Criminal Law," pp. 1221, 1237.

48. With reference to white-collar crime generally, see Wheeler, Mann, and Sarat, *Sitting in Judgement* p. 166–74.

49. von Hirsch, *Doing Justice*, p. 38.

50. Yoder, "Comment: Criminal Sanctions," p. 45.

51. William Chambliss, "Types of Deviance and the Effectiveness of the Legal Sanction," *Wisconsin Law Review* (Summer 1967), pp. 703–19.

52. For an excellent analysis of how judges interpret deterrence concerns in their sentencing decisions for white-collar criminals, see Wheeler, Mann, and Sarat, *Sitting in Judgement*, pp. 133–44.

53. John Braithwaite and Gilbert Geis, "On Theory and Action for Corporate Crime Control," *Crime and Delinquency* (April 1982), pp. 301–2.

54. Ibid., p. 301.

55. Chambliss, "Types of Deviance," p. 714.

CHAPTER 2

1. Braithwaite and Geis, "On Theory and Action," pp. 303–5.

2. August Bequai, "White-Collar Plea Bargaining," *Trial Magazine* (July 1979), pp. 38–41.

3. For a partial list of corporate offenses and their sanctions, see Orland, "Reflections on Corporate Crime," p. 510n.63. See also Clinard and Yeager, *Corporate Crime*, Appendix B, pp. 330–33. There are a few offenses that carry longer prison terms. These statues pertain mostly to bribery and fraud and financial crimes such as insider trading. The United States Sentencing Commission is now constructing sentencing guidelines for corporate crimes. These guidelines reflect the prevailing view that sentences for corporate crimes should be raised. See United States Sentencing Commission, *Sentencing Guidelines and Policy Statements* (Washington, D.C.: U.S. Printing Office, 1987).

4. Robert Ogren, "The Ineffectiveness of the Criminal Sanction in Fraud and Corruption Cases: Losing the Battle against

White-Collar Crime," *American Criminal Law Review* 11 (1973), pp. 959–88.

5. See, for example, William Chambliss, *Criminal Law in Action* (Santa Barbara, Calif.: Hamilton, 1975).

6. John Hagan, Ilene Nagel, and Celesta Albonetti, "The Differential Sentencing of White-Collar Offenders in Ten Federal District Courts," *American Sociological Review* 45 (1980), pp. 802–20. See also Hagan and Nagel, "White-Collar Crime, White-Collar Time: The Sentencing of White-Collar Offenders in the Southern District of New York," *American Criminal Law Review* 20 (1982), pp. 199–229. In addition, the authors found a considerable difference in sentencing patterns between white-collar-offense groups, with a higher rate of confinement for offenses that involved violations of public trust.

7. Stanton Wheeler, David Weisburd, and Nancy Bode, "Sentencing the White-Collar Offender: Rhetoric and Reality," *American Sociological Review* 47 (1982), pp. 641–59.

8. Gilbert Geis, "Criminological Perspectives on Corporate Regulation: Review of Recent Research," in *Corrigible Corporations and Unruly Law*, ed. Brent Fisse and Peter French (San Antonio: Trinity University Press, 1985), pp. 63–84. See also Hagan and Nagel, "White-Collar Crime, White-Collar Time," pp. 199–229.

9. Geis, "Criminological Perspectives," pp. 75–77.

10. Kenneth Mann, Stanton Wheeler, and Austin Sarat, "Sentencing the White-Collar Offender," *American Criminal Law Review* 17 (1980), p. 491. See also Wheeler, Mann, and Sarat, *Sitting in Judgement*.

11. *Yale Law Journal*, "Note: Increasing Community Control Over Corporate Crime—A Problem in the Law of Sanctions," *Yale Law Journal* 71 (1961), pp. 280–306.

12. See, for example, Ogren, "Ineffectiveness of the Criminal Sanction," pp. 959–68.

13. Richard Posner, "Optimal Sentences for White-Collar Criminals," *American Criminal Law Review* 17 (1980), pp. 409–18; William Breit and Kenneth Elzinga, "Antitrust Penalties and Attitudes Toward Risk: An Economic Analysis," *Harvard Law Review* 86 (1975), pp. 693–713. See also John Coffee, Jr., "Corporate Crime and Punishment: A Non-Chicago View of the Economics of Criminal Punishment," *American Criminal Law Review* 17 (1980), pp. 419–76.

14. See Donna Sammons Carpenter and John Feloni, *The Fall of the House of Hutton* (New York: Henry Holt, 1989).

15. For example, see *Yale Law Journal*, "Note: Increasing Community Control," pp. 280–306; Geis, "Criminal Penalties," pp. 377–92; Ogren, "Ineffectiveness of the Criminal Sanction," pp. 959–88; and Yoder, "Comment: Criminal Sanctions," pp. 40–58.

16. Posner, "Optimal Sentences for White-Collar Criminals," 409–18; Coffee, "Corporate Crime and Punishment," pp. 419–76.

17. Breit and Elzinga, "Antitrust Penalties" pp. 693–713.

18. Christopher Stone, "Controlling Corporate Misconduct," *Public Interest* 48 (1977), pp. 57–58.

19. Ibid., p. 57. See also Clinard and Yeager, *Corporate Crime*, p. 48; and Richard M. Cyert and James G. March, *A Behavioral Theory of the Firm* (Englewood Cliffs, N.J.: Prentice Hall, 1963).

20. *Yale Law Journal*, "Note: Increasing Community Control," p. 3.

21. Stone, "Controlling Corporate Misconduct," p. 58.

22. Ibid.

23. Ibid., p. 59.

24. John Coffee, Jr., " 'No Soul to Damn, No Body to Kick': An Unscandalized Inquiry into the Problem of Corporate Punishment," *Michigan Law Review* 70 (1981): p. 410.

25. Yoder, "Comment: Criminal Sanctions," p. 49.

26. Francis Allen, "Regulation by Indictment: The Criminal Law as an Instrument of Economic Control" (McInally Memorial Lecture at the University of Michigan, 1978), p. 13.

27. Melvin A. Eisenberg, "The Legal Roles of Shareholders and Management in Modern Corporate Decisionmaking," *California Law Review* 57 (1969), p. 33; Stone, *Where the Law Ends*, pp. 47–48; J. A. C. Hetherington, "When the Sleeper Wakes: Reflections on Corporate and Shareholders Rights," *Hofstra Law Review* 8 (1979), pp. 183–255.

28. See Coffee, "No Soul to Damn," pp. 401–2, and Fisse, "Reconstructing Corporate Criminal Law," pp. 1219–20.

29. See Fisse, "Reconstructing Corporate Criminal Law," pp. 1213–21, and Yoder, "Comment: Criminal Sanctions," p. 48.

30. John Coffee, Jr., "Making the Punishment Fit the Corporation: The Problem of Finding the Optimal Corporate Criminal Sanction," *Northern Illinois University Law Review* 3 (1980), pp. 15–20; Coffee, "No Soul to Damn," pp. 413–24.

31. Coffee, "No Soul to Damn," p. 390.

32. Coffee, "Making the Punishment Fit," p. 19.

33. Ibid., pp. 15–16.

34. Ibid., p. 16.

35. Ibid., p. 19.

36. Ibid., p. 20.

37. Fisse, "Reconstructing Corporate Criminal Law," pp. 1233–37.

38. Ibid., pp. 1235–36.

39. Coffee, "Making the Punishment Fit," p. 20.

40. See, to name a few, United States v. Atlantic Richfield Co., 465 F. 2nd 58 (7th Cir. 1972); Apex Oil v. United States, 530 F. 2nd 1291 (8th Cir.), cert. denied, 429 U.S. 827 (1976); and United States v. Nu-Triumph, Inc., F. 2nd 594 (9th Cir. 1974).

41. See *Yale Law Journal*, "Note: Structural Crime," and *Yale Law Journal*, "Note: Judicial Intervention," pp. 513–37.

42. See Coffee, "No Soul to Damn," pp. 448–59; see also *Yale Law Journal*, "Note: Structural Crime," p. 365.

43. *Yale Law Journal*, "Note: Structural Crime," p. 547.

44. Ibid., pp. 549–52.

45. See Stone, "The Place of Enterprise Liability," pp. 1–77.

46. According to John Kenneth Galbraith: "In the American business code nothing is as iniquitous as government interference in the affairs of the corporation." *The New Industrial State*, 3d ed. (New York: New American Library, 1978), p. 81.

47. See Mann, Wheeler, and Austin, "Sentencing the White-Collar Offender," p. 482.

48. See Fisse, "Reconstructing Corporate Criminal Law," p. 1226.

49. Ibid., p. 1228.

50. Ibid., p. 1229.

51. Brent Fisse and John Braithwaite, *The Impact of Publicity on Corporate Offenders* (Albany: State University of New York Press, 1983), p. 232.

52. Ibid., pp. 232–33.

53. Ibid., p. 312.

54. Reagan wrote a letter to the *Los Angeles Times* stating that he found General Electric to "operate with the highest of Principles—higher I might add than some of the elements of Government bent on destroying business." From Geis, "Criminal Penalties for Corporate Criminals," *Criminal Law Bulletin* 8 (1972), p. 381.

CHAPTER 3

1. The major accounts of desert can be found in John Kleinig, *Punishment and Desert* (The Hague: Martinus Nijhoff, 1973); Andrew von Hirsch, *Doing Justice*, and *Past or Future Crimes: Deservedness and Dangerousness in the Sentencing of Criminals* (New Brunswick: Rutgers University Press, 1985); and Richard G. Singer, *Just Deserts: Sentencing Based on Equity and Desert* (Cambridge, Mass.: Ballinger, 1979). See also C. W. K. Mundle, "Punishment and Desert," *Philosophical Quarterly* 4 (1954), pp. 216–228, and K. G. Armstrong, "The Retributivist Hits Back," *Mind* 70 (1961), pp. 471–90.

2. Andrew von Hirsch, "Recent Trends in American Criminal Sentencing Theory," *Maryland Law Review* 42 (1983), pp. 7–10.

3. Twentieth Century Fund, Task Force on Criminal Sentencing, *Fair and Certain Punishment* (New York: McGraw-Hill, 1976), p. 98.

4. For a good review of these reforms, see von Hirsch, "Recent Trends," pp. 6–36.

5. American Friends Service Committee, *Struggle for Justice* (New York: Hill and Wang, 1971), p. 99.

6. John Monahan, "The Prevention of Violence," in *Community Mental Health and the Criminal Justice System*, ed. John Monahan (New York: Pergamon Press, 1976).

7. Ibid., p. 15.

8. For a general review, see Todd Clear and Vincent O'Leary, *Controlling the Offender in the Community* (Lexington, Mass.: Lexington Books, 1983), pp. 35–43.

9. Don M. Gottfredson, "Screening for Risk: A Comparison of Methods," *Criminal Justice and Behavior* 7 (1980), p. 315.

10. See, for example, David F. Greenberg, "The Correctional Effects of Corrections," in *Corrections and Punishment*, ed. David F. Greenberg (Beverly Hills, Calif.: Sage, 1977), pp. 111–48; and Roger Hood and Richard Sparks, *Key Issues in Criminology* (New York: McGraw-Hill, 1970), pp. 215–35. For a more extensive bibliography, see Gross and von Hirsch, eds., *Sentencing*, p. 186.

11. Douglas Lipton, Robert Martinson, and Judith Wilks, *The Effectiveness of Correctional Treatment: A Survey of Treatment Evaluation Studies* (New York: Praeger, 1975).

12. See Panel on Research on Rehabilitative Techniques, "Report," in *The Rehabilitation of Criminal Offenders: Problems and Prospects* (Washington, D.C.: National Academy of Sciences, 1979), pp. 1–147.

13. For example, see James Q. Wilson, "What Works? Revisited: New Findings on Rehabilitation," *Public Interest* 61 (Fall 1980); pp. 3–17.

14. Twentieth Century Fund, *Fair and Certain Punishment*, p. 102.

15. Ibid., p. 102.

16. Ibid., pp. 101–6.

17. von Hirsch, "Recent Trends," p. 15.

18. Ibid., p. 8.

19. American Bar Association, Task Force on Sentencing Alternatives and Procedures, *Sentencing Alternatives and Procedures*, 2d ed. (Washington, D.C.: American Bar Association, 1979).

20. For a critique of the Bar Association's report, see Andrew von Hirsch, "Utilitarian Sentencing Resuscitated: The American Bar As-

sociation's Second Report on Criminal Sentencing," *Rutgers Law Review* 33 (Spring 1981), pp. 772–89.

21. American Bar Association, *Sentencing Alternatives and Procedures*, 2d ed., pp. 73–74.

22. See, for example, Richard Posner, *Economic Analysis of Law*, 2d ed. (Boston: Little, Brown, 1977), and Ernest van den Haag, "Punishment as a Device for Controlling the Crime Rate," *Rutgers Law Review* 33 (1981), pp. 706–20.

23. According to this argument, offenders are deterred more by the certainty of serving some time in jail than by the severity of a stiff term seldom imposed.

24. von Hirsch, "Recent Trends," p. 18.

25. See, for example, Coffee, "No Soul to Damn," pp. 386–459.

26. von Hirsch, "Utilitarian Sentencing Resuscitated," p. 772.

27. See von Hirsch, *Past or Future Crimes*, pp. 51–53.

28. Henry M. Hart, Jr., writes, "A crime is conduct, which if duly shown to have taken place, will incur a formal and solemn pronouncement of the moral condemnation of the community." Henry M. Hart, Jr., "The Aims of the Criminal Law," *Law and Contemporary Problems* 23 (1958), p. 405.

29. von Hirsch, *Past or Future Crimes*, pp. 63–66.

30. Oregon, Minnesota, Washington, and Pennsylvania have each established sentencing provisions that incorporate desert principles in various forms. See von Hirsch, *Past or Future Crimes*, p. 11.

31. Ibid., pp. 167–74.

32. Ibid., pp. 34–37.

33. Ibid., pp. 40–43.

34. Singer, *Just Deserts*, p. 27.

35. von Hirsch, *Past or Future Crimes*, pp. 44–46.

36. For instance, in *Past or Future Crimes* von Hirsch grapples with the use of categorical incapacitation as a guide to locate these points. Ibid., pp. 147–67.

37. Ibid., pp. 44–45.

CHAPTER 4

1. Brent Fisse notes, "It is unfashionable to regard retribution as a legitimate, much less significant, justification for punishing corporations." Fisse, "Reconstructing Corporate Criminal Law," p. 1167.

2. See, for example, John Braithwaite, "Challenging Just Deserts: Punishing White-Collar Criminals," *Journal of Criminal Law and Criminology* 73 (1982), pp. 729–31; and Yoder, "Comment: Criminal Sanctions," p. 47.

3. Fisse, "Reconstructing Corporate Criminal Law," pp. 1176–80; and Kadish, "Some Observations," pp. 435–40.

4. See Richard Wasserstrom, "Retribution and the Theory of Punishment," *Journal of Philosophy* 75 (1978), p. 601.

5. H. L. A. Hart, "Prolegomenon to the Principles of Punishment," in H. L. A. Hart, *Punishment and Responsibility* (New York: Oxford University Press, 1968), pp. 1–4.

6. Ibid., p. 3.

7. I refer principally to the works of von Hirsch, *Past or Future Crimes*, and *Doing Justice*; and to Singer, *Just Deserts*. See also Andrew von Hirsch, "Desert and White-Collar Criminality: A Response to Dr. Braithwaite," *Journal of Criminal Law and Criminology* 73 (1982), pp. 1164–66.

8. See *Harvard Law Review*, "Developments in the Law," pp. 1231–41.

9. For instance, see Yoder, "Comment: Criminal Sanctions," pp. 44–47.

10. H. L. A. Hart, "Prolegomenon," p. 8.

11. Richard Posner, *The Economics of Justice* (Cambridge: Harvard University Press, 1981), p. 208.

12. Ibid., p. 215.

13. Jeffrie Murphy, *Retribution, Justice, and Therapy* (Dordrecht, the Netherlands: Reidel, 1979) p. 77.

14. For an overview of Kant, see Jeffrie Murphy, *Kant: The Philosophy of Right* (London: Macmillan, 1970), pp. 140–44; for a summary of Hegel and Bradley with regard to retributive punishment, see Edmund Pincoff, "The Classical Debate," in *The Rationale for Punishment* (New York: Humanities Press, 1966), pp. 9–17. See also Murphy, *Retribution, Justice, and Therapy*; John Finnis, "The Restoration of Retribution," *Analysis* 32 (1972), pp. 131–35.

15. Pincoff, "The Classical Debate," p. 8.

16. Immanuel Kant, *Rechtslehre*, Part Second, 49, trans. E. Hastie (Edinburgh, 1887), pp. 195–97.

17. Kant suggests, for example, that crime consists of a hindrance of freedom. Since freedom should not be hindered, a constraint must then be placed on that hindrance. Punishment represents, therefore, "a hindering of a hindrance of freedom." Pincoff, "The Classical Debate" p. 9.

18. Armstrong, "The Retributivist Hits Back," p. 36.

19. Pincoff, "The Classical Debate," pp. 9–15.

20. See John Rawls, "Legal Obligation and the Duty of Fair Play," in *Law and Philosophy*, ed. Sidney Hook (New York: New York University Press, 1964), pp. 3–18.

21. Murphy, *Retribution, Justice, and Therapy*, p. 77. Emphasis added.

22. Murphy refers to those taking this position as "rule utilitarians." Ibid., p. 78.

23. See H. L. A. Hart, "Murder and the Principles of Punishment," in *Punishment and Responsibility*, p. 79.

24. Finnis, *Natural Law and Natural Rights*, p. 132.

25. Ibid., p. 263.

26. Yoder, "Comment: Criminal Sanctions," p. 47.

27. Braithwaite, "Challenging Just Deserts," pp. 730–31.

28. von Hirsch, *Past or Future Crimes*, pp. 58–59.

29. Ibid., p. 59. See also Murphy, "Marxism and Retribution," in *Retribution, Justice, and Therapy*, pp. 93–115.

30. von Hirsch, *Past or Future Crimes*, p. 59.

31. Fisse, "Reconstructing Corporate Criminal Law," p. 1171.

32. See Stone, *Where the Law Ends*, p. 184.

33. For a discussion of the expressive function of punishment, see Joel Feinberg, "The Expressive Function of Punishment," in *Doing and Deserving: Essays in the Theory of Responsibility* (Princeton: Princeton University Press, 1970), pp. 95–118. See also von Hirsch, *Past or Future Crimes*.

34. Feinberg, "The Expressive Function of Punishment," pp. 101–5.

35. Ibid., p. 102.

36. von Hirsch, *Past or Future Crimes*, p. 52.

37. Ibid., p. 53.

38. Feinberg, "Justice and Personal Desert," in *Doing and Deserving*, p. 81.

39. See Andrew von Hirsch, "Neoclassicism, Proportionality, and the Rationale for Punishment: Thoughts on the Scandinavian Debate," *Crime and Delinquency* 29 (1983), pp. 52, 67–69.

40. See, for example, *Harvard Law Review*, "Developments in the Law," pp. 1233–35; Thurman Arnold, "Antitrust Law Enforcement, Past and Future," *Law and Contemporary Problems* 7 (1940), pp. 5, 11; Ball and Friedman, "Criminal Sanctions," p. 219; Kadish, "Some Observations," *University of Chicago Law Review* 30 (1963), pp. 423, 425–26, 436; and Kovel, "A Case for Civil Penalties," pp. 153, 154–55.

41. Yoder, "Comment: Criminal Sanctions," p. 42.

42. See, for example, Clinard and Yeager, *Corporate Crime;* John Johnson and Jack Douglas, eds., *Crime at the Top: Deviance in Business and the Professions* (Philadelphia: Lippincott, 1978); John E. Conklin, *Illegal but Not Criminal: Business Crime in America* (Englewood Cliffs, N.J.: Prentice Hall, 1977); and James W. Coleman, *The Criminal Elite: The Sociology of White-Collar Crime* (New York: St. Martin's Press, 1985).

43. For a description of the Richardson-Merrell case, see Stanford J. Unger, "Get Away with What You Can," in Robert L. Heilbroner,

ed., *In the Name of Profit: Profiles in Corporate Irresponsibility* (New York: Doubleday, 1972), pp. 106–27. The Firestone Tire case can be found in Coleman, *The Criminal Elite*, pp. 41–42. A description of the Equity Funding scam can be found in William Blundell, "Equity Funding: I Did It for the Jollies," reprinted in Johnson and Douglas, *Crime at the Top*, pp. 153–85.

44. Francis Cullen et al., "Public Support for Punishing White-Collar Crime: Blaming the Victim Revisited?" *Journal of Criminal Justice* 11 (1983), pp. 481–93; Laura Schrager and James Short, "How Serious a Crime? Perceptions of Organizational and Common Crimes," in Geis and Stotland, eds., *White-Collar Crime*, pp. 14–31; P. G. Sinden, "Perceptions of Crime in Capitalist America: The Question of Consciousness Manipulation," *Sociological Focus* 13 (1980), pp. 75–85; and Conklin, *Illegal but Not Criminal*.

45. Cullen et al., "Public Support," p. 482.

46. Kadish, "Some Observations," p. 306.

47. Cullen et al., "Public Support," p. 486.

48. Hart, "Aims of the Criminal Law," p. 405.

49. See Cullen, Maakestadt, and Cavender, *Corporate Crime Under Attack;* Howard Becker, *Outsiders* (New York: Free Press, 1963); and Jack Katz, "The Social Movement against White-Collar Crime," in Egon Bitner and Sheldon Messinger, eds., *Criminology Review Yearbook*, vol. 2. (Beverly Hills, Calif.: Sage, 1980), pp. 161–84.

50. Victoria Swigert and Ronald Farrell, "Corporate Homicide: Definitional Processes in the Creation of Deviance," *Law and Society Review* 15 (1980–81), pp. 161–82.

CHAPTER 5

1. Andrew von Hirsch, "Doing Justice: The Principles of Commensurate Deserts," in Gross and von Hirsch, eds., *Sentencing*, p. 245.

2. H. L. A. Hart, *Punishment and Responsibility,* p. 114.

3. There are, of course, utilitarian arguments limiting the distribution of punishments to those who have voluntarily committed the offense. This discussion will be limited, however, to the retributive rationale, which emphasizes notions of individual justice.

4. Brent Fisse notes that whether it is possible to attribute fault to a corporation on a genuinely corporate, yet workable, basis has proven to be the "blackest hole" in the theory of corporate criminal law. "Reconstructing Corporate Criminal Law," p. 1183.

5. See Elkins, "Corporations and the Criminal Law," pp. 73–129.

6. Gerhard O. W. Mueller, "*Mens Rea* and the Corporation," *University of Pittsburgh Law Review* 19 (1957), pp. 38–41.

7. Ibid., p. 38.

8. Ibid.

9. *Wall Street Journal*, 7 February 1985, sec. 1, pps. 2, 5, 22.

10. Lawrence Haworth, "Do Organizations Act?" *Ethics* (October 1959), pp. 59–63.

11. Ibid., pp. 60–61.

12. Mueller, "*Mens Rea* and the Corporation," p. 39.

13. Peter French, *Collective and Corporate Responsibility* (New York: Columbia University Press, 1984), p. 181.

14. See Coffee, "No Soul to Damn," p. 399.

15. See Mueller, "*Mens Rea* and the Corporation," p. 39.

16. Ibid., p. 41.

17. American Law Institute, *Model Penal Code* (Philadelphia: American Law Institute, 1962), pp. 35–37.

18. From this perspective, the corporate conscience is evident not only in the *acts* of high managerial officials, but also in the acts *authorized* by such officials.

19. L. H. Leigh, "Criminal Liability of Corporations and Other Groups," *Ottawa Law Review* 9 (1977), p. 253.

20. French, *Collective and Corporate Responsibility*, p. 41.

21. Ibid.

22. Ibid., p. 48.

23. Ibid., p. 53.

24. Ibid., p. 7.

25. Ibid., p. 44.

26. The manner in which such a method may be used to determine culpability factors in questions of seriousness needs much greater attention and is not within the scope of this study.

27. The Kepone case is a clear example of this. Evidence indicates that high managerial officials were not aware of the incident until the news became public; once they were, however, corrective steps were taken immediately. Fisse, "Reconstructing Corporate Criminal Law," pp. 1199–1200.

28. French, *Collective and Corporate Responsibility*, p. 184.

29. Ibid.

30. Fisse, "Reconstructing Corporate Criminal Law," p. 1202n.291.

31. Ibid., p. 1183.

32. Brent Fisse, "The Duality of Corporate and Individual Criminal Liability," in Hochstedler, ed., *Corporations as Criminals* (Beverly Hills, Calif.: Sage, 1984), pp. 69–84.

33. John Coffee, Jr., notes that efforts by commentators "seeking

to fashion retributive justifications and anthropomorphic analogies only compounds the legal fiction of corporate personality with the legal fiction of corporate mens rea, but worse yet, it blinds us to the real issue of how to make deterrence work where the offender is an organization." "No Soul to Damn," p. 448.

34. French, *Collective and Corporate Responsibility*, p. 186.

35. Leigh, "Criminal Liability of Corporations," p. 275.

36. Hyman Gross, *A Theory of Criminal Justice* (New York. Oxford University Press, 1979), p. 372.

37. Ibid., pp. 349–53.

38. One point needs to be addressed here. Much of this book has involved the applicability of desert principles to corporate entities. It reflects a process of deduction from the principles that guide the punishment of natural persons. It has been pointed out, however, that such a deduction is not required in special cases of corporations unless there is some logical principle which requires that corporations be treated differently from natural persons. This suggestion appears to make sense. Yet, as I have tried to demonstrate in this chapter, much of the reluctance by those writing on corporate punishment toward the role of desert is due precisely to misgivings about the deducibility of general principles to corporate entities. Whether such a deduction is required or not, it does help to clarify the issues. Memorandum from Richard F. Sparks pointing this out.

CHAPTER 6

1. See von Hirsch, *Doing Justice*, pp. 77–88.

2. For a review of the literature on perceptions of offense seriousness and their implications, see Thorsten Sellin and Marvin Wolfgang, *The Measurement of Delinquency* (New York: Wiley, 1964; reprint, Montclair, N.J.: Patterson Smith, 1978); Francis Cullen, Bruce G. Link, and C. W. Polanzi, "The Seriousness of Crime Revisited: Have Attitudes toward White-Collar Crime Changed?" *Criminology* 20 (1982), pp. 83–102; Robert Figlio, "The Seriousness of Offenses: An Evaluation of Offenders and Non-Offenders," *Journal of Criminal Law and Criminology* 75 (1984), pp. 459–73; Terance Meithe, "Public Consensus on Crime Seriousness: Normative Structure or Methodological Artifact," *Criminology* 20 (1982), pp. 516–20, and "Types of Consensus in Public Evaluations of Crime: An Illustration of Strategies for Measuring 'Consensus,'" *Journal of Criminal Law and Criminology* 75 (1984), pp. 459–73; Marc Riedel, "Perceived Circumstances, Inferences of Intent, and Judgments of Offense Seriousness," *Journal of Criminal Law and Criminology* 66

(1975), p. 201; Peter Rossi and J. Patrick Henry, "Seriousness: A Measure for All Purposes?" in *Handbook of Criminal Justice Evaluation*, ed. Malcolm W. Klein and Katherine Teilman (Beverly Hills, Calif.: Sage, 1980); Peter Rossi et al., "The Seriousness of Crime: Normative Structure and Individual Differences," *American Sociological Review* 39 (1974), pp. 224–37; Peggy Shelley and Richard Sparks, "Crime and Punishment," paper presented at the annual meeting of the American Society of Criminology, San Francisco, 5–8 November 1980; and Richard F. Sparks, Hazel Genn, and David Dodd, *Surveying Victims: A Study of The Measurement of Criminal Victimization, Perceptions of Crime and Attitudes to Criminal Justice* (London: Wiley, 1977).

3. Sellin and Wolfgang, *The Measurement of Delinquency*; Leslie Sebba, "Some Exploration in the Scaling of Penalties," *Journal of Research in Crime and Delinquency* 15 (1978), p. 274, and "Further Explorations in the Scaling of Penalties," *British Journal of Criminology* 23 (July 1984), p. 221; and Shelley and Sparks, "Crime and Punishment."

4. Cullen, Link, and Polanzi, "The Seriousness of Crime Revisited," p. 93.

5. Yet, evidence from Sebba indicates that these factors are very relevant in the determination of offense seriousness. In a replication of the Baltimore study, Meithe found that more than 71 percent of the variation in mean seriousness ratings was explained by the type of harm, intentionality of the actor, and whether the description implied victim consent (Meithe, "Types of Consensus," p. 468n.32.) Riedel found that the degree of harm (e. g., the extent of the physical injury or monetary loss) was an important consideration, while Sykes and West found that respondents took under consideration the extent of harm, the intent of the actor, and the motive and the characteristics of the offender and the victim in their assessment of severity. (Riedel, "Perceived Circumstances," p. 211. See also Leslie Sebba, "Is Mens Rea a Component of Perceived Offense Seriousness?" *Journal of Criminal Law and Criminology* 71, no. 2 (1980), pp. 124–35.)

6. Richard F. Sparks, unpublished paper delivered at Sterling Forest Conference Center, Tuxedo, New York, November 1978.

7. von Hirsch, *Past or Future Crimes*, p. 66.

8. Gerhard O. W. Mueller, "Criminal Theory: An Appraisal of Jerome Hall's Studies in Jurisprudence and Criminal Theory," *Indiana Law Journal* 34 (1959), pp. 216, 220.

9. For a summary of the development of the concept of harm in Great Britain and Germany, see Albin Eser, "The Principle of 'Harm' in the Concept of Crime: A Comparative Analysis of the Criminally

Protected Legal Interests," *Duquesne University Law Review* 4 (1965), pp. 349–70, and Jerome Hall, *General Principles of Criminal Law*, 2d ed. (Indianapolis: Bobbs-Merrill, 1960), pp. 212–46.

10. Hall, *General Principles of Criminal Law*, p. 217.

11. Ibid.

12. From Eser, "The Principle of 'Harm,' " p. 371; see also Mueller, "Criminal Theory," p. 220.

13. John Kleinig, "Crime and the Concept of Harm," *American Philosophical Quarterly* 15 (January 1978), p. 31.

14. Ibid.

15. Joel Feinberg, *Harm to Others: The Moral Limits of the Criminal Law* (New York: Oxford University Press, 1984), pp. 55–64.

16. Ibid., p. 62.

17. Both von Hirsch and Feinberg, while acknowledging the relevance of this question, consider generic interests to be largely interdependent to one another. See von Hirsch, *Past or Future Crimes*, p. 69, and Feinberg, *Harm to Others*, pp. 37, 57–58.

18. von Hirsch, *Past or Future Crimes*, p. 67.

19. Feinberg, *Harm to Others*, pp. 37–45, 185–214.

20. von Hirsch, *Past or Future Crimes*, pp. 67–71.

21. Feinberg, *Harm to Others*, p. 42.

22. Ibid., p. 206.

23. von Hirsch, *Past or Future Crimes*, p. 70.

24. Feinberg, *Harm to Others*, p. 207.

25. Clearly, not all will view these interests similarly. To the extent that this is true, the law incorporates the notion of "standard interests." As Joel Feinberg writes: "The criminal law must employ general rules that are applicable to everyone, and are reasonably simple. Multiform interests must be protected by uniform rules. The problem is solved by the positing of a 'standard person' who can be protected from standard forms of harm to 'standard interests.' The law gains greatly in convenience and clarity and loses little or nothing in justice by 'presuming' that certain interests are possessed in common by everyone and then imposing uniform duties of noninterference with them. The standard person has certain standard welfare interests including, for example, interests in continued life, health, economic sufficiency and political liberty. Laws can be generally put: harms to these interests, at least, must be protected." *Harm to Others*, p. 188.

26. von Hirsch, *Past or Future Crimes*, p. 69.

27. Feinberg, *Harm to Others*, pp. 204–5, 217.

28. C. Wright Mills, *The Power Elite* (New York: Oxford University Press, 1956), p. 95.

29. Jeremy Bentham, *An Introduction to the Principles of Morals and Legislation*, ed. J. H. Burns and H. L. A. Hart (London: Methuen, 1982), p. 189.

30. Focusing on the aggregate harm of a typical case of price-fixing as a basis for assessing seriousness is not the same as focusing on the aggregate harm of all instances of price-fixing and the total costs of those harms to society. As von Hirsch has noted, seriousness is "represented by the loss typically stemming from a single actor's consequences, since he is responsible only for his own acts and not the acts of others who are engaged in similar conduct." "Desert and White-Collar Criminality," p. 1169.

31. Feinberg, *Harm to Others*, pp. 204–6, 216.

32. For a discussion of the question of utility and corporate activity and the need to consider this with regard to liability of corporations for criminal behavior, see Michael Metzger, "Corporate Criminal Liability for Defective Products: Policies, Problems, and Prospects," *Georgetown Law Journal* 73, no. 1 (1985), pp. 74–86.

33. Andrew von Hirsch notes: "Rating harmfulness involves *judgment*. Since the definitions of the welfare or security interests are couched in general and imprecise terms, one can expect some disagreement about whether and to what extent a given type of criminal act infringes on such interests. But such imprecision almost inevitably exists in grading situations: grading is typically a judgment exercise in which the graders utilize general criteria that guide but do not automatically determine the rating decision. The individual graders may differ in the ratings they assign, but the differences seldom are pervasive enough to cast doubt on the grading enterprise." *Past or Future Crimes*, p. 71.

34. Feinberg, *Harm to Others*, p. 203.

CHAPTER 7

1. von Hirsch, *Past or Future Crimes*, p. 72.

2. National Commission on Reform of Federal Criminal Laws, *Working Papers* (Washington, D.C., 1970), pp. 119–20; see also Peter Low, John Calvin Jeffries, Jr., and Richard Bonnie, *Criminal Law: Cases and Materials* (Mineola, N.Y.: Foundation Press, 1982), pp. 205–6.

3. The same commission commented that "the courts have endowed the requirement of 'willfulness' with the capacity to take on whatever meaning seems appropriate in the statutory context." *Working Papers*, p. 206.

4. See United States v. United States Gypsum Co., 98 S. Court 2864 (1978).

5. Low, Jeffries, and Bonnie, *Criminal Law*, pp. 205–6.

6. "Model Penal Code Culpability Provisions," section 2.02, *Model Penal Code*, defines the requirements as follows:

A person acts *purposefully* with respect to a material element of an offense when: 1. if the element involves the nature of his conduct or a result thereof, it is his conscious object to engage in conduct of that nature or to cause such a result; and 2. if the element involves the attendant circumstances, he is aware of the existence of such circumstances or he believes or hopes they exist.

An offender acts *knowingly* when: 1. if the element involves the nature of his conduct or the attendant circumstances, he is aware that his conduct is of that nature or that such circumstances exist; and 2. if the element involves a result of his conduct, he is aware that it is practically certain that his conduct will cause such a result.

An offender acts *recklessly* when he consciously disregards a substantial and unjustifiable risk that the material element exists or will result from his conduct. The risk must be of such a nature and degree that, considering the nature and purpose of the actor's conduct and the circumstances known to him, its disregard involves a gross deviation from the standard of conduct that a law-abiding person would observe in the actor's situation.

A person acts *negligently* . . . when he should be aware of a substantial and unjustifiable risk that a material element exists or will result from his conduct. The risk must be of such a nature and degree that the actor's failure to perceive it, considering the nature and purpose of his conduct and the circumstances known to him, involves a gross deviation from the standard of care that a reasonable person would observe in the actor's situation.

7. von Hirsch, *Past or Future Crimes*, p. 72.

8. See pages 78–80 *supra*.

9. *Model Penal Code*, section 207 4 (C), 1962. This concept is not entirely new, as it has been recognized in courts in Great Britain, Australia, New Zealand, and Canada. See Fisse, "Reconstructing Corporate Criminal Law," p. 1187.

10. See pages 81–83 *supra*.

11. French, *Collective and Corporate Responsibility*, p. 41.

12. Ibid., p. 51.

13. French writes: "The idea of a rule of recognition is borrowed from H. L. A. Hart's version of legal positivism. For Hart, a recognition rule is a fundamental secondary rule in a legal system that ultimately determines what laws are valid in that system. In other words, a demonstration of the validity of any law is incomplete if it does not terminate in the citation of a rule of recognition. To show that a law is valid one may need to uncover a chain of validity back to the basic recognition rule of the system." Ibid., p. 52. See also Hart, *The Concept of Law* (Oxford: Oxford University Press, 1961), ch. 6.

14. *Wall Street Journal*, 4 December 1985, sec. 1, p. 2.

15. Ibid., p. 4.

16. Clinard and Yeager, *Corporate Crime*, p. 44.

17. French, *Collective and Corporate Responsibility*, p. 51.

18. Peter Drucker, *The Concept of the Corporation* (New York: Crowell, 1972), pp. 36–37.

19. French, *Collective and Corporate Responsibility*, pp. 54–56.

20. The Sharp case is described in detail in Fisse and Braithwaite, *The Impact of Publicity*, pp. 115–23.

21. Ibid., p. 337n.23.

22. Ibid.

23. Ibid., p. 121.

24. "American Airlines Pays $1.5 Million Fine after FAA Cites Maintenance Violations," *Wall Street Journal*, 30 September 1985, sec. 2, p. 42.

25. Ibid., p. 5.

26. Although the original rationale for not prosecuting the corporate agents was the lack of evidence indicating individual personal knowledge of the activity, recent evidence indicates that the prevailing sentiment of those involved not to prosecute individuals was based on practical rather than evidentiary concerns. According to the Assistant U.S. Attorney in charge of the investigation, "I made the recommendation that [not to prosecute individuals] would be in the best interest of the country and the entire banking system to avoid lengthy litigation," "U.S. Official Testifies on Not Prosecuting Hutton Executives," *Wall Street Journal*, 12 December 1985, sec. 1, p. 5.

27. "Hutton Memo Shows Approval of Overdrafts," *Wall Street Journal*, 20 June 1985, sec. 1, p. 2.

28. Ibid.

29. "Hutton Ex-President Ball Was Informed of Bank Overdrafts, Documents Show," *Wall Street Journal*, 1 July 1985, sec. 1, p. 3.

30. "Hutton Memo Shows Approval," p. 2.

31. John Braithwaite, *Corporate Crime in the Pharmaceutical Industry* (London: Routledge and Kegan Paul, 1984), pp. 69–70.

32. Gross, *A Theory of Criminal Justice* pp. 87–88.

33. See Metzger, "Corporate Criminal Liability" p. 54.

34. *Harvard Law Review*, "Note: Developments in the Law" p. 1265.

35. Ibid., p. 1266.

36. This view differs substantially from that taken by the law outside the corporate realm, where there is a general unwillingness to impose criminal liability for knowing of a crime but failing to prevent it. Ibid., p. 1268, especially note 130.

37. See, for example, Stone, *Where the Law Ends*, p. 60; Metzger, "Corporate Criminal Liability," p. 54; Clinard and Yeager, *Corporate Crime*, p. 279. *Yale Law Journal*, "Note: Structural Crime," pp. 357–58.

38. Stone, *Where the Law Ends*, p. 60.

39. See, for example, Herbert A. Simon, *Administrative Behavior*, 2d ed. (New York: Macmillan, 1957), pp. 123–71, and Fred Luthans, *Organizational Behavior*, 4th ed. (New York: McGraw-Hill, 1985), pp. 257–65.

40. *Yale Law Journal*, "Note: Structural Crime," p. 353.

41. S. 1437, *supra* note 6, section 403 (c).

42. Ibid.

43. Ibid., section 302 (c).

44. See Clinard and Yeager, *Corporate Crime*, p. 44, and Braithwaite, "Challenging Just Deserts," p. 754.

45. Fisse, "Reconstructing Corporate Criminal Law," p. 1197.

46. Reactive corporate fault has been used to determine assessment and mitigation of civil penalties. See 42 U.S.C. Section 6928(a) 1976. See also *Yale Law Journal*, "Note: The Statutory Injunction as an Enforcement Weapon of Federal Agencies," *Yale Law Journal* 57 (1948), pp. 1028–29, and Fisse, "Reconstructing Corporate Criminal Law," p. 1195n.253.

47. Fisse, "Reconstructing Corporate Criminal Law," p. 1196.

48. Coffee, "No Soul to Damn," p. 446.

49. Singer, *Just Deserts*, ch. 5, and George Fletcher, *Rethinking Criminal Law* (Boston: Little, Brown, 1982), pp. 460–66.

50. von Hirsch, *Past or Future Crimes*, ch. 7, and "Desert and Previous Convictions in Sentencing," *Minnesota Law Review* 5 (1982), pp. 591–634.

51. von Hirsch, "Desert and Previous Convictions," pp. 613–15. (For the sake of simplicity, the masculine pronoun is used throughout this discussion to refer to both male and female offenders.)

52. Ibid., p. 614.

53. von Hirsch, *Past or Future Crimes*, pp. 82–83.

54. Ibid., pp. 83–84.

55. Ibid., p. 72.

56. Ibid., pp. 71–74.

57. Martin Wasik, "Excuses at the Sentencing Stage," *Criminal Law Review* (1983), pp. 450–65.

CHAPTER 8

1. von Hirsch, *Past or Future Crimes*, p. 39.

2. Ibid., pp. 38–46.

3. Ibid., p. 40.

4. Ibid., p. 36.

5. Ibid., p. 92.

6. Ibid., pp. 92–93.

7. Ibid., p. 93.

8. Ibid., pp. 160–66.

9. Kleinig, *Punishment and Desert*, ch. 5, n. 37.

10. See, in particular, *Yale Law Journal*, "Note: Structural Crime," pp. 353–75, and "Note: Judicial Intervention," pp. 513–37.

11. 40 F. Supp. 122 (E.D.Va. 1976), No. 78–30, Slip op. (D. Conn. 1978), respectively. See also Brent Fisse, "Community Service as a Sanction against Corporations," *Wisconsin Law Review* (1981), pp. 970–1017.

12. Christopher Stone, "A Slap on the Wrist for the Kepone Mob," *Business and Society Review* 22 (1977), pp. 4–11.

13. *New York Times*, 2 June 1978, sec. D, p. 1.

14. Fisse, "Community Service as a Sanction," p. 975.

15. Ibid., p. 978.

16. Ibid., p. 983.

17. Ibid., p. 981.

18. Roger Hood, "Criminology and Penal Change: A Case Study of the Nature and Impact of Some Recent Advice to Governments," in *Crime, Criminology, and Public Policy*, ed. Roger Hood (New York: Free Press, 1974), pp. 375, 408–12.

19. Yet, as with community-service orders, structural intervention can be levied through corporate criminal probation as well. See James R. Farrand, "Ancillary Remedies in SEC Civil Enforcement Suits," *Harvard Law Review* 89 (1979), pp. 1805–14.

20. *Yale Law Journal*, "Note: Structural Crime," p. 366.

21. Fisse and Braithwaite, *The Impact of Publicity*.

22. See pp. 38–39 *supra*.

23. Fisse and Braithwaite, *The Impact of Publicity*, p. 112.

24. Fisse and Braithwaite do talk about the range of impact on prestige in terms of the financial consequences incurred by the corporation, but prestige is a more complicated notion that affects a broad variety of corporate interests not directly tied to finances.

25. Ibid., p. 294.

26. See Metzger, "Corporate Criminal Liability," p. 65, and Stone, "Controlling Corporate Misconduct," p. 58.

27. For a discussion of the general deterrent impact of fines, see chapter 2, *supra*. See also Christopher Kennedy, "Criminal Sentences for Corporations: Alternative Fining Mechanisms," *California Law Review* (March 1985), p. 443.

28. See, for example, Jane Mallor and Barry Roberts, "Punitive Damages: Toward a Principled Approach," *Hastings Law Journal* 31 (January 1980), pp. 639–70, and John Bagby, Norman Miller, and Michael Solt, "The Determination of Compensatory Damages: A Valuation Framework," *American Business Law Journal* 22 (1984), pp. 1–39.

29. Joel Feinberg, "Expressive Function of Punishment," p. 118.

30. Coffee, "No Soul to Damn," p. 402.

31. French, *Collective and Corporate Responsibility*, p. 189; Coffee, "No Soul to Damn," p. 402.

32. French, *Collective and Corporate Responsibility*, p. 189.

33. *Pennsylvania Law Review*, "Notes—Fines and Fining," *University of Pennsylvania Law Review* 101 (1953), pp. 1024–25.

34. Ibid., p. 1024.

35. Hans Thornstedt, "The Day-Fine System in Sweden," *Criminal Law Review* (1975), p. 308. The advantages of the day-fine system have been outlined as follows: "1. Fines are imposed more equitably. 2. Since they are levied according to wealth, there is a greater probability of actual payment and, thus, of increased revenues. 3. Whatever deterrent effects fines have will be augmented, especially in regard to the wealthy but also for all persons, because of the increased certainty of collections. 4. Although some or all of these standards (wealth, income, productive capacity and dependents) are consciously or unconsciously applied at the present time by many judges on a 'hunch' basis, this type of statute specifies them concretely and forces all courts to take cognizance of them. Flexibility of sentence is retained and even expanded by allowing both the gravity of the offense and the particular status of the offender to be considered." *Pennsylvania Law Review*, "Notes—Fines and Fining," p. 1026.

36. Letter from Nils Jareborg providing these figures.

37. *Pennsylvania Law Review*, "Notes—Fines and Fining," p. 1026; Thornstedt, "The Day-Fine System in Sweden," p. 309.

38. Thornstedt, "The Day-Fine System in Sweden," p. 310.

39. Ibid., p. 309.

40. See, for example, Toscony Provision Company v. Block, 538 F. Supp. 318 (D.N.J. 1982).

41. Kennedy, "Criminal Sentences for Corporations, pp. 445–446n.10.

42. See, for example, "Kidder Peabody Is Censured by the SEC for Allegedly Misusing Client Securities," *Wall Street Journal*, 11 February 1986, sec. 1, p. 7; and "Big Board Disciplines Four Companies and 19 People for Alleged Violations," *Wall Street Journal*, 12 February 1986, sec. 2, p. 4.

43. von Hirsch, *Past or Future Crimes*, pp. 154–59.

44. Ibid., pp. 95–100. See also Andrew von Hirsch, "Constructing Guidelines for Sentencing: The Critical Choices for the Minnesota Sentencing Guidelines Commission," *Hamline Law Review* 5 (1982), pp. 164–215.

45. See Jacqueline Cohen, "Incapacitation as a Strategy for Crime Control: Possibilities and Pitfalls," in *Crime and Justice: An Annual Review of Research*, ed. Michael Tonry and Norval Morris, vol. 5 (Chicago: University of Chicago Press, 1983), pp. 1–84.

46. von Hirsch, *Doing Justice*, p. 93.

CHAPTER 9

1. von Hirsch, *Past or Future Crimes*, pp. 31–37.

2. See French, *Collective and Corporate Responsibility*, p. 186, and Coffee, "No Soul to Damn," p. 448.

3. Haworth, "Do Organizations Act?" *Ethics* (October 1959), p. 60.

4. French, *Collective and Corporate Responsibility*, p. 41.

5. See pp. 91–95 *supra*.

6. See Feinberg, *Harm to Others*, pp. 55–64.

7. Wheeler, Mann, and Sarat, *Sitting in Judgement*, pp. 168–74.

8. See pp. 97–103 *supra*.

9. See chapter 7.

10. American Law Institute, "Model Penal Code Culpability Provisions," Section 2.02, *Model Penal Code*.

11. See pp. 133–37 *supra*.

12. See pp. 142–44 *supra*.

13. von Hirsch, *Past or Future Crimes*, pp. 40–43.

14. Ibid., pp. 43–46.

15. See chapter 8.

16. See pp. 166–71 *supra*.

17. This is not a problem unique to desert. Utilitarian-based punishments seek to prevent behaviors deemed offensive as well, and certainly the efforts to deter offenders will be part and product of the preferences of those who have the power to make laws. Yet, there is a subtle difference between utilitarian-based punishments and reprobation-based punishments. While the former is designed for the most part to prevent the offensive activity, the latter takes on an additional function—to *encourage*, directly or indirectly, the kind of morality deemed important to society. As von Hirsch notes:

> The role of punishment in reinforcing law-abiding citizens' moral inhibitions must derive from the more fundamental role of express-

ing judgments about the wrongfulness of certain conduct. Why should anybody take his or her moral cues from the criminal law? The answer has to be that penal law embodies a considered judgment that the punished behavior is wrong, and that people should take that judgment into account in forming their own standards of right and wrong. [*Past or Future Crimes*, p. 51.]

18. Take as another example the gas leak in Bhopal, India. Obviously, for harm considered alone, the offense is of the most serious kind. Yet, a system that punishes the taking of human life as the most serious transgression encounters difficulty when one offense kills ten people and another kills two thousand. Few would agree that punishing both equally is fair, and it is uncertain whether such differences could be adequately covered in the range of punishments provided for aggravating circumstances.

19. von Hirsch, *Past or Future Crimes*, pp. 65 66.
20. Clinard and Yeager, *Corporate Crime*, p. 44.
21. See, for example, Shapiro, *Wayward Capitalists*, pp. 135–65.
22. French, *Collective and Corporate Responsibility*, p. 186.
23. Kleinig, *Punishment and Desert*, ch. 7.
24. Ibid.
25. Wheeler, Mann, and Sarat, *Sitting in Judgement*, p. 176.
26. Ayn Rand, *The Fountainhead* (New York: Signet Books, 1943).

Bibliography

American Bar Association. Task Force on Sentencing Alternatives and Procedures. *Sentencing Alternatives and Procedures.* 2d ed. Washington, D.C.: American Bar Association, 1979.

American Friends Service Committee. *Struggle for Justice.* New York: Hill and Wang, 1971.

American Law Institute. *Model Penal Code.* Philadelphia: American Law Institute, 1962.

Armstrong, K. G. "The Retributivist Hits Back." *Mind* 70 (1961): 471–90.

Arnold, Thurman. "Antitrust Law Enforcement, Past and Future." *Law and Contemporary Problems* 7 (1940): 5–23.

Bagby, John, Norman Miller, and Michael Solt. "The Determination of Compensatory Damages: A Valuation Framework." *American Business Law Journal* 22 (1984): 1–39.

Ball, Harry, and Lawrence Friedman. "Criminal Sanctions in the Enforcement of Economic Legislation: A Sociological View." *Stanford Law Review* 17 (1965): 197–223.

Becker, Howard. *Outsiders.* New York: Free Press, 1963.

Bentham, Jeremy. *An Introduction to the Principles of Morals and Legislation.* Edited by J. H. Burns and H. L. A. Hart. London: Methuen, 1982.

Bequai, August. "White-Collar Plea Bargaining." *Trial Magazine* (July 1979): 38–41.

Braithwaite, John. "Challenging Just Deserts: Punishing White-Collar Criminals." *Journal of Criminal Law and Criminology* 73 (1982): 723–63.

——— . *Corporate Crime in the Pharmaceutical Industry.* London: Routledge and Kegan Paul, 1984.

Braithwaite, John, and Gilbert Geis. "On Theory and Action for Corporate Crime Control." *Crime and Delinquency* (April 1982): 292–314.

Breit, William, and Kenneth Elzinga. "Antitrust Penalties and Attitudes Toward Risk: An Economic Analysis." *Harvard Law Review* 86 (1975): 693–713.

219

Bibliography

Carpenter, Donna Sammons, and John Feloni. *The Fall of the House of Hutton*. New York: Henry Holt, 1989.

Chambliss, William. *Criminal Law in Action*. Santa Barbara, Calif.: Hamilton, 1975.

———. "Types of Deviance and the Effectiveness of the Legal Sanction." *Wisconsin Law Review* (Summer 1967): 703–19.

Clear, Todd, and Vincent O'Leary. *Controlling the Offender in the Community*. Lexington, Mass.: Lexington Books, 1983.

Clinard, Marshall, and Peter Yeager. *Corporate Crime*. New York: Free Press, 1980.

Clinard, Marshall, et al. *Illegal Corporate Behavior*. Washington, D.C.: U.S. Government Printing Office, 1979.

Coffee, John, Jr. "Corporate Crime and Punishment: A Non-Chicago View of the Economics of Criminal Punishment." *American Criminal Law Review* 17 (1980): 419–476.

———. "Making the Punishment Fit the Corporation: The Problem of Finding the Optimal Corporate Criminal Sanction." *Northern Illinois University Law Review* 3 (1980): 3–26.

———. " 'No Soul to Damn, No Body to Kick': An Unscandalized Inquiry into the Problem of Corporate Punishment." *Michigan Law Review* 79 (1981): 386–459.

Cohen, Jacqueline. "Incapacitation as a Strategy for Crime Control: Possibilities and Pitfalls." In *Crime and Justice: An Annual Review of Research*, edited by Michael Tonry and Norval Morris, vol. 5, 1–84.

Coleman, James W. *The Criminal Elite: The Sociology of White-Collar Crime*. New York: St. Martin's Press, 1985.

Conklin, John E. *Illegal but Not Criminal: Business Crime in America*. Englewood Cliffs, N.J.: Prentice-Hall, 1977.

Cullen, Francis, Bruce G. Link, and C. W. Polanzi. "The Seriousness of Crime Revisited: Have Attitudes toward White-Collar Crime Changed?" *Criminology* 20 (1982): 83–102.

Cullen, Francis, William Maakestadt, and Gray Cavender. *Corporate Crime Under Attack: The Ford Pinto Case and Beyond*. Cincinnati: Anderson Press, 1987.

Cullen, Francis, et al. "Public Support for Punishing White-Collar Crime: Blaming the Victim Revisited?" *Journal of Criminal Justice* 11 (1983): 481–93.

Cyert, Richard M., and James G. March. *A Behavioral Theory of the Firm*. Englewood Cliffs, N.J.: Prentice-Hall, 1963.

Drucker, Peter. *The Concept of the Corporation*. New York: Crowell, 1972.

Bibliography

Edelhertz, Herbert. *The Nature, Impact, and Prosecution of White-Collar Crime*. Washington, D.C.: U.S. Government Printing Office, 1970.

Eisenberg, Melvin A. "The Legal Roles of Shareholders and Management in Modern Corporate Decisionmaking." *California Law Review* 57 (1969): 1–118.

Elkins, James R. "Corporations and the Criminal Law: An Uneasy Alliance." *Kentucky Law Journal* 65 (1976): 73–129.

Eser, Albin. "The Principle of 'Harm' in the Concept of Crime: A Comparative Analysis of the Criminally Protected Legal Interests." *Duquesne University Law Review* 4 (1965): 345–417.

Farrand, James R. "Ancillary Remedies in SEC Civil Enforcement Suits." *Harvard Law Review* 89 (1979): 1805–14.

Feinberg, Joel. "The Expressive Function of Punishment." In *Doing and Deserving: Essays in the Theory of Responsibility*, 95–118. Princeton: Princeton University Press, 1970.

——— . *Harm to Others: The Moral Limits of the Criminal Law*. New York: Oxford University Press, 1984.

——— . "Justice and Personal Desert." In *Doing and Deserving: Essays in the Theory of Responsibility*, 55–87. Princeton: Princeton University Press, 1970.

Figlio, Robert. "The Seriousness of Offenses: An Evaluation of Offenders and Non-Offenders." *Journal of Criminal Law and Criminology* 75 (1984): 459–73.

Fine, Sam. "The Philosophy of Enforcement." *Food, Drug, and Cosmetic Law Journal* 31 (1976): 324–37.

Finnis, John M. "The Restoration of Retribution." *Analysis* 32 (1972): pp. 131–35.

Fisse, Brent. "Community Service as a Sanction against Corporations." *Wisconsin Law Review* (1981): 970–1017.

——— . "The Duality of Corporate and Individual Criminal Liability." In *Corporations as Criminals*, edited by Ellen Hochstedler, 69–84. Beverly Hills, Calif.: Sage, 1984.

——— . "Reconstructing Corporate Criminal Law: Deterrence, Retribution, Fault, and Sanctions." *Southern California Law Review* 56 (1983): 1141–1246.

Fisse, Brent, and John Braithwaite. *The Impact of Publicity on Corporate Offenders*. Albany: State University of New York Press, 1983.

Fisse, Brent, and Peter French, eds. *Corrigible Corporations and Unruly Law*. San Antonio: Trinity University Press, 1985.

Fletcher, George. *Rethinking Criminal Law*. Boston: Little, Brown, 1982.

221

Bibliography

French, Peter A. *Collective and Corporate Responsibility*. New York: Columbia University Press, 1984.

Galbraith, John Kenneth. *The New Industrial State*. 3d ed. New York: New American Library, 1978.

Geis, Gilbert. "Criminal Penalties for Corporate Criminals." *Criminal Law Bulletin*. 8 (1972): 377–92.

———. "Criminological Perspectives on Corporate Regulation: Review of Recent Research." In *Corrigible Corporations and Unruly Law*, edited by Brent Fisse and Peter French, 63–84. San Antonio: Trinity University Press, 1985.

Geis, Gilbert, and Ezra Stotland, eds. *White-Collar Crime: Theory and Research*. Beverly Hills, Calif.: Sage, 1980.

Gottfredson, Don M. "Screening for Risk: A Comparison of Methods." *Criminal Justice and Behavior* 7 (1980): 302–25.

Greenberg, David F. "The Correctional Effects of Corrections." In *Corrections and Punishment*, edited by David F. Greenberg. Beverly Hills, Calif.: Sage, 1977.

Gross, Hyman. *A Theory of Criminal Justice*. New York: Oxford University Press, 1979.

Gross, Hyman, and Andrew von Hirsch, eds. *Sentencing*. New York: Oxford University Press, 1981.

Hagan, John, and Ilene Nagel. "White-Collar Crime, White-Collar Time: The Sentencing of White-Collar Offenders in the Southern District of New York." *American Criminal Law Review* 20 (1982): 199–229.

Hagan, John, Ilene Nagel, and Celesta Asbonetti. "The Differential Sentencing of White-Collar Offenders in Ten Federal District Courts." *American Sociological Review* 45 (1980): 802–20.

Hall, Jerome. *General Principles of Criminal Law*. 2d ed. Indianapolis: Bobbs-Merrill, 1960.

Hart, H. L. A. *The Concept of Law*. Oxford: Oxford University Press, 1961.

———. "Murder and the Principles of Punishment." In *Punishment and Responsibility*, 54–89. New York: Oxford University Press, 1968.

———. "Prolegomenon to the Principles of Punishment." In *Punishment and Responsibility*, 1–27. New York: Oxford University Press, 1968.

Hart, Henry M., Jr. "The Aims of the Criminal Law." *Law and Contemporary Problems* 23 (1958): 401–13.

Harvard Law Review. "Developments in the Law—Corporate Crime: Regulating Corporate Behavior through Criminal Sanctions." *Harvard Law Review* 92 (1979): 1227–1375.

Bibliography

Haworth, Lawrence. "Do Organizations Act?" *Ethics* (October 1959): 59–63.

Heilbroner, Robert L., ed. *In the Name of Profit: Profiles in Corporate Irresponsibility*. New York: Doubleday, 1972.

Hetherington, J. A. C. "When the Sleeper Wakes: Reflections on Corporate and Shareholders Rights." *Hofstra Law Review* 8 (1979): 183–255.

Hood, Roger. "Criminology and Penal Change: A Case Study of the Nature and Impact of Some Recent Advice to Governments." In *Crime, Criminology, and Public Policy*, edited by Roger Hood, 375–418. New York: Free Press, 1974.

Hood, Roger, and Richard Sparks. *Key Issues in Criminology*. New York: McGraw-Hill, 1970.

Johnson, John, and Jack Douglas, eds. *Crime at the Top: Deviance in Business and the Professions*. Philadelphia: Lippincott, 1978.

Kadish, Sanford. "Some Observations on the Use of Criminal Sanctions in the Enforcement of Economic Regulations." *University of Chicago Law Review* 30 (1963): 423–49.

Kant, Immanuel. *Rechtslehre*. Part second, 49. Trans. E. Hastie. Edinburgh, 1887.

Katz, Jack. "The Social Movement against White-Collar Crime." In *Criminology Review Yearbook*, edited by Egon Bitner and Sheldon Messinger. Vol. 2, 161–84. Beverly Hills, Calif.: Sage, 1980.

Kennedy, Christopher. "Criminal Sentences for Corporations: Alternative Fining Mechanisms." *California Law Review* (March 1985): 443–82.

Kleinig, John. "Crime and the Concept of Harm." *American Philosophical Quarterly* 15 (January 1978): 27–36.

—————. *Punishment and Desert*. The Hague: Martinus Nijhoff, 1973.

Kovel, Alexander. "A Case for Civil Penalties: Air Pollution Control." *Journal of Urban Law* 46 (1969): 153–97.

Kramer, Ronald. "Corporate Criminality, the Development of an Idea." In *Corporations as Criminals*, edited by Ellen Hochstedler. Beverly Hills, Calif.: Sage, 1984.

Leigh, L. H. "Criminal Liability of Corporations and Other Groups." *Ottawa Law Review* 9 (1977): 253–87.

Lipton, Douglas, Robert Martinson, and Judith Wilks. *The Effectiveness of Correctional Treatment: A Survey of Treatment Evaluation Studies*. New York: Praeger, 1975.

Low, Peter, John Calvin Jeffries, Jr., and Richard Bonnie. *Criminal Law: Cases and Materials*. Mineola, N.Y.: Foundation Press, 1982.

Bibliography

Luthans, Fred. *Organizational Behavior.* 4th ed. New York: McGraw-Hill, 1985.

Mallor, Jane, and Barry Roberts. "Punitive Damages: Toward a Principled Approach." *Hastings Law Journal* 31 (January 1980): 639–70.

Mann, Kenneth, Stanton Wheeler, and Austin Sarat. "Sentencing the White-Collar Offender." *American Criminal Law Review* 17 (1980): 479–500.

Meithe, Terance. "Public Consensus on Crime Seriousness: Normative Structure or Methodological Artifact." *Criminology* 20 (1982): 516–26.

——— . "Types of Consensus in Public Evaluations of Crime: An Illustration of Strategies for Measuring 'Consensus.' " *Journal of Criminal Law and Criminology* 75 (1984): 459–73.

Metzger, Michael. "Corporate Criminal Liability for Defective Products: Policies, Problems, and Prospects." *Georgetown Law Journal* 73, no. 1 (1985): 1–88.

Mills, C. Wright. *The Power Elite.* New York: Oxford University Press, 1956.

Monahan, John. "The Prevention of Violence." In *Community Mental Health and the Criminal Justice System,* edited by John Monahan. New York: Pergamon Press, 1976.

Mueller, Gerhard O. W. "Criminal Theory: An Appraisal of Jerome Hall's Studies in Jurisprudence and Criminal Theory." *Indiana Law Journal* 34 (1959): 206–20.

——— . "*Mens Rea* and the Corporation." *University of Pittsburgh Law Review* 19 (1957): 21–50.

Mundle, C. W. K. "Punishment and Desert." *Philosophical Quarterly* 4 (1954): 216–28.

Murphy, Jeffrie. *Kant: The Philosophy of Right.* London: Macmillan, 1970.

——— . *Retribution, Justice, and Therapy.* Dordrecht, the Netherlands: Reidel, 1979.

National Academy of Sciences, Panel on Research on Rehabilitative Techniques. *The Rehabilitation of Criminal Offenders: Problems and Prospects.* Washington, D.C.: National Academy of Sciences (1979).

National Commission on Reform of Federal Criminal Laws. *Working Papers.* Washington, D.C.: 1970.

New York Times. 2 June 1978, sec. D, p. 1.

Ogren, Robert. "The Ineffectiveness of the Criminal Sanction in Fraud and Corruption Cases: Losing the Battle against White-Collar Crime." *American Criminal Law Review* 11 (1973): 959–88.

Bibliography

Orland, Leonard. "Reflections on Corporate Crime: Law in Search of Theory and Scholarship." *American Criminal Law Review* 17 (1980): 501–21.

Parisi, Nicolette. "Theories of Corporate Criminal Liability." In *Corporations as Criminals*, edited by Ellen Hochstedler, 41–68. Beverly Hills, Calif.: Sage, 1984.

Pennsylvania Law Review. "Notes—Fines and Fining." *University of Pennsylvania Law Review* 101 (1953): 1013–30.

Pincoff, Edmund. "The Classical Debate." In *The Rationale for Punishment*. New York: Humanities Press, 1966.

Posner, Richard. *Economic Analysis of Law*. 2d ed. Boston: Little, Brown, 1987.

———. *The Economics of Justice*. Cambridge, Mass.: Harvard University Press, 1981.

———. "Optimal Sentences for White-Collar Criminals." *American Criminal Law Review* 17 (1980): 409–18.

———. "A Statistical Study of Antitrust Enforcement." *Journal of Law and Economics* 13 (1970): 365–419.

Rand, Ayn. *The Fountainhead*. New York: Signet Books, 1943.

Rawls, John. "Legal Obligation and the Duty of Fair Play." In *Law and Philosophy*, edited by Sidney Hook, 3–12. New York: New York University Press, 1964.

Riedel, Marc. "Perceived Circumstances, Inferences of Intent, and Judgments of Offense Seriousness." *Journal of Criminal Law and Criminology* 66 (1975): 201–8.

Rossi, Peter, and J. Patrick Henry. "Seriousness: A Measure for All Purposes?" In *Handbook of Criminal Justice Evaluation*, edited by Malcolm W. Klein and Katherine Teilman. Beverly Hills, Calif.: Sage, 1980.

Rossi, Peter, et al. "The Seriousness of Crime: Normative Structure and Individual Differences." *American Sociological Review* 39 (1974): 224–37.

Schrager, Laura, and James Short. "How Serious a Crime? Perceptions of Organizational and Common Crimes. In *White-Collar Crime: Theory and Research*, edited by Gilbert Geis and Ezra Stotland, 14–27. Beverly Hills, Calif.: Sage, 1980.

Sebba, Leslie. "Further Explorations in the Scaling of Penalties." *British Journal of Criminology* 23 (1984): 221–46

———. "Is Mens Rea a Component of Perceived Offense Seriousness?" *Journal of Criminal Law and Criminology* 71, no. 2 (1980): 124–35.

———. "Some Exploration in the Scaling of Penalties." *Journal of Research in Crime and Delinquency* 15 (1978): 274–89.

Bibliography

Sellin, Thorsten, and Marvin Wolfgang. *The Measurement of Delinquency.* New York: Wiley, 1964. Reprint. Montclair, N.J.: Patterson Smith, 1978.

Shapiro, Susan. *Wayward Capitalists: Target of the Securities and Exchange Commission.* New Haven: Yale University Press, 1984.

Simon, Herbert A. *Administrative Behavior.* 2d ed. New York: Macmillan, 1957.

Sinden, P. G. "Perceptions of Crime in Capitalist America: The Question of Consciousness Manipulation." *Sociological Focus* 13 (1980): 75–85.

Singer, Richard G. *Just Deserts: Sentencing Based on Equity and Desert.* Cambridge, Mass.: Ballinger, 1979.

Sparks, Richard F., Hazel Genn, and David Dodd. *Surveying Victims: A Study of the Measurement of Criminal Victimization, Perceptions of Crime and Attitudes to Criminal Justice.* London: Wiley, 1977.

Stone, Christopher. "Controlling Corporate Misconduct." *Public Interest* 48 (1977): 55–71.

——— . "The Place of Enterprise Liability in the Control of Corporate Conduct." *Yale Law Journal* 90 (1980): 1–77

——— . "A Slap on the Wrist for the Kepone Mob." *Business and Society Review* 22 (1977): 4–11.

——— . *Where the Law Ends: The Social Control of Corporate Behavior.* New York: Harper & Row, 1975.

Swigert, Victoria, and Ronald Farrell, "Corporate Homicide: Definitional Processes in the Creation of Deviance." *Law and Society Review* 15 (1980–81): 161–82.

Thornstedt, Hans. "The Day-Fine System in Sweden." *Criminal Law Review* (1975): 307–12.

Twentieth Century Fund. Task Force on Criminal Sentencing. *Fair and Certain Punishment.* New York: McGraw-Hill, 1976.

United States Sentencing Commission. *Sentencing Guidelines and Policy Statement.* Washington, D.C.: U.S. Government Printing Office, 1987.

van den Haag, Ernest. "Punishment as a Device for Controlling the Crime Rate." *Rutgers Law Review* 33 (1981): 706–20.

von Hirsch, Andrew. "Constructing Guidelines for Sentencing: The Critical Choices for the Minnesota Sentencing Guidelines Commission." *Hamline Law Review* 5 (1982): 164–215.

——— . "Desert and Previous Convictions in Sentencing." *Minnesota Law Review* 5 (1982): 591–634.

Bibliography

————. "Desert and White-Collar Criminality: A Response to Dr. Braithwaite." *Journal of Criminal Law and Criminology* 73 (1982): 1164–75.

————. *Doing Justice: The Choice of Punishments.* New York: Hill and Wang, 1976.

————. "Neoclassicism, Proportionality, and the Rationale for Punishment: Thoughts on the Scandinavian Debate." *Crime and Delinquency* 29 (1983): 52–70.

————. *Past or Future Crimes: Deservedness and Dangerousness in the Sentencing of Criminals.* New Brunswick: Rutgers University Press, 1985.

————. "Recent Trends in American Criminal Sentencing Theory." *Maryland Law Review* 42 (1983): 6–36.

————. "Utilitarian Sentencing Resuscitated: The American Bar Association's Second Report on Criminal Sentencing." *Rutgers Law Review* 33 (Spring 1981): 772–89.

Wasik, Martin. "Excuses at the Sentencing Stage." *Criminal Law Review* (1983): 450–65.

Wasserstrom, Richard. "Retribution and the Theory of Punishment." *Journal of Philosophy* 75 (1978): 601–23.

Wheeler, Stanton, Kenneth Mann, and Austin Sarat. *Sitting in Judgement: The Sentencing of White-Collar Criminals.* New Haven: Yale University Press, 1988.

Wheeler, Stanton, David Weisburd, and Nancy Bode. "Sentencing the White-Collar Offender: Rhetoric and Reality." *American Sociological Review* 47 (1982): 641–59.

Wilson, James Q. "What Works? Revisited: New Findings on Rehabilitation." *Public Interest* 61 (Fall 1980): 3–17.

Yale Law Journal. "Note: Increasing Community Control Over Corporate Crime—A Problem in the Law of Sanctions." *Yale Law Journal* 71 (1961): 280–306.

————. "Note: Judicial Intervention and Organizational Theory: Changing Bureaucratic Behavior and Policy." *Yale Law Journal* 89 (1979): 513–37.

————. "Note: The Statutory Injunction as an Enforcement Weapon of Federal Agencies." *Yale Law Journal* 57 (1948): 1028–29.

————. "Note: Structural Crime and Institutional Rehabilitation: A New Approach to Corporate Sentencing." *Yale Law Journal* 89 (1979): 353–75.

Yoder, Stephen. "Comment: Criminal Sanctions for Corporate Illegality." *Journal of Criminal Law and Criminology* 69 (1978): 40–58.

Index

Index

Index

Harm (*cont.*)
    109–10, 112, 113–14, 181, 184–
    85, 209n. 25, 210n. 33, 217n. 18
Hart, H. L. A., 54–55, 56, 122,
    211n. 13
Hart, Henry, 70
Haworth, Lawrence, 77–78
Hegel, G. W. F., 57, 58
Highway safety, 9
Hood, Roger, 155

*Impact of Publicity on Corporate
    Offenders, The* (Fisse and
    Braithwaite), 159
Imprisonment, 61, 152, 197n. 3,
    198n. 6; vs. adverse publicity,
    160; deterrent effect of, 16, 20–
    22, 31, 39, 40, 197n. 3, 198n. 6;
    and prediction, 44, 45–47; and
    proportionality, 50, 149, 173,
    183, 187; and resource
    constraints, 151, 174, 187; and
    suspension of business activities
    compared, 171, 172, 173
Incapacitation, 13–14, 46, 174, 177
Indemnification, 27
Individual liability, xiv, 26–27, 85–
    86, 178–79; aggravating and miti-
    gating circumstances, 142–44,
    173, 182; and intent, 7–8, 86–87,
    133–38, 181, 185–86, 194nn.
    17–21; and scaling of punish-
    ment, 173–75. *See also* Fines;
    Imprisonment
Injunctions, 10, 14, 34–35
Insanity defense, 49
Insider trading, 25, 197n. 3
Intent, 48, 94, 118–19, 185–86,
    210n. 3; and acquiescence, 135,
    212n. 36; and civil vs. criminal
    sanctions, 12, 195n. 32; and cor-
    porate liability, 6, 10, 76–79, 84,
    86–87, 207n. 33; and corpora-
    tion's prior record, 142; and indi-
    vidual liability, 7–8, 86–87, 133–

38, 181, 185–86, 194nn. 17–21;
    Model Penal Code standards of,
    118–19, 134, 145, 181, 210–11n.
    6; reactive, 138, 213n. 46; and
    sentencing of individual agents,
    133–38; vs. strict liability, 7, 87–
    88, 118, 145, 194n. 15. *See also*
    CID structure; Culpability
Iran-Contra affair, 24

Judges, discretion of, 43, 45, 46,
    47, 154, 189
Justice Department, 11, 12

Kadish, Sanford, 70
Kant, Immanuel, 57–58, 59, 203n.
    17
Kennedy v. Mendoza-Martinez,
    195n. 32
Kepone, 154, 206n. 27
Kleinig, John, xii, 97, 109, 150, 186
Knowledge, 7, 94, 118, 134, 181,
    194n. 17; and acquiescence, 135,
    212n. 36; and CID structure,
    129–31, 186; definition of, 211n.
    6

Leigh, H. L., 81
Love Canal, 3
Luthans, Fred, 136

Mala in se, 67
Mala prohibita, 67. *See also* Regu-
    latory offenses
Managers, 32–33, 79, 137. *See also*
    Individual liability
Mann, Kenneth, 180, 181, 189–90
Meithe, Terance, 208n. 5
Mens rea. See Intent
Mer/29, 68
Mexico, 166
Mills, C. Wright, 105
Minnesota, 202n. 30
Misfeasance, 5–6

232

Index

Mitigating circumstances: for corporations, 138–42, 182, 213n. 46; for individuals, 142–44, 173, 182
Model Penal Code: on corporate liability, 79–81, 84, 120; degrees of fault under, 118–19, 134, 145, 181, 210–11n. 6
Monetary fines. *See* Fines
Motive, 49
Mueller, Gerhard O. W., 76–77, 78–79, 95–96
Murphy, Jeffrie, 57, 58–59, 203n. 22

Nagel, Ilene, 20
National Academy of Sciences, 45
National Commission on Reform of Federal Criminal Laws, 118
Necessity defense, 49, 143
Negligence, 7, 86, 94, 118, 119; and CID structure, 129, 132–33, 186; definition of, 194n. 18, 211n. 6; and sentencing, 134, 181
New Haven Community Betterment Fund, 154
New York Central and Hudson River Railroad Co. v. the United States, 7
Nonfeasance, 5, 6, 76

Occupational-health offenses, 24
Officers, corporate, 6, 26, 80. *See also* Individual liability
Ogren, Robert, 20
Olin Mathieson Corporation, 154
Oregon, 202n. 30
Orland, Leonard, 195n. 23

Parole boards, 43, 45, 47
Paton, J., 131
Pennsylvania, 202n. 30
Phillips Petroleum Co., 28
Political corruption, 106
Polls, 92–95, 180, 208n. 5

Pollution, 10, 24, 106, 110, 112–13, 184
Prediction, 43, 44, 45–47
Preventive detention, 44. *See also* Imprisonment
Price-fixing, xiii, 24, 69, 70, 105, 210n. 30
Probation, 35–37, 50, 154, 214n. 19
Product safety, 9, 10
Proportionality, xiv; and adverse publicity, 160–61; of cash fines, 162–63, 165–66; and community service, 156–57; and criminal sanctions for individual agents, 173–75; of day fines, 166–71; and deterrence, 47; ordinal and cardinal, 49–50, 147, 148–51, 153, 182–83; and rehabilitation and prediction, 45–47; and revenge, 56; and structural intervention, 158; and suspension of business activities, 172–73
Publicity, 12, 15; as criminal sanction, 38–39, 40, 159–61, 183, 187, 200n. 54
Purpose, 118, 129, 134, 135, 181, 186; definition of, 211n. 6

Rand, Ayn, 190
Rawls, John, 58
Reactive corporate fault, 138–39, 213n. 46
Reagan, Ronald, 39, 200n. 54
Recalls, product, 9, 195n. 27
Recidivism, 44, 174
Recklessness, 7, 118, 119; and CID structure, 129, 131–33, 186; definition of, 194n. 18, 211n. 6; and sentencing, 134, 137–38, 181
Refuse Act, 194n. 15
Regulatory offenses: and definition of corporate crime, 4, 195n. 23; enforcement options for, 8–13; moral opprobrium of, xi, 53, 69, 71; and risk of harm, 7, 106–8, 110–11

233

Index